Food Sovereignty

Food Sovereignty

Towards democracy in localized food systems

Michael Windfuhr and Jennie Jonsén
FIAN-International

Published by ITDG Publishing
The Schumacher Centre for Technology and Development, Bourton Hall
Bourton-on-Dunsmore, Rugby, Warwickshire, CV23 9QZ, UK.
www.itdgpublishing.org.uk

© ITDG Publishing 2005

First published in 2005

ISBN 1-85339-610-9

A catalogue record for this book is available from the British Library.

ITDG Publishing is the publishing arm of Intermediate Technology Development
Group Ltd. Our mission is to build the skills and capacity of people in developing
countries through the dissemination of information in all forms, enabling them
to improve the quality of their lives and that of future generations.

Typeset by J&L Composition, Filey, North Yorkshire
Printed in Great Britain by Antony Rowe Ltd., Chippenham, Wiltshire

Contents

Preface

ITDG commissioned this paper by FIAN as a contribution to the discourse on Food Sovereignty, the rapidly developing food and agriculture policy framework. In a world plagued simultaneously and perversely by hunger and obesity, rational policies are overdue for governing the way food is grown, processed and traded, and how the benefits of the world's food systems are shared.

Most food in the world is grown, collected and harvested by more than a billion small-scale farmers, pastoralists and artisanal fisherfolk. This food is mainly sold, processed, resold and consumed locally, thereby providing the foundation of people's nutrition, incomes and economies across the world. At a time when halving world poverty and eradicating hunger are at the forefront of the international development agenda, reinforcing the diversity and vibrancy of local food systems should also be at the forefront of the international policy agenda. Yet the rules that govern food and agriculture at all levels – local, national and international – are designed *a priori* to facilitate not local, but international trade. This reduces diversity and concentrates the wealth of the world's food economies in the hands of ever fewer multinational corporations, while the majority of the world's small-scale food producers, processors, local traders and consumers including, crucially, the poor and malnourished, are marginalized.

In this paper, Michael Windfuhr shows how the Food Sovereignty policy framework addresses this dilemma. The policy framework starts by placing the perspective and needs of the majority at the heart of the global food policy agenda and embraces not only the control of production and markets, but also the Right to Food, people's access to and control over land, water and genetic resources, and the use of environmentally sustainable approaches to production. What emerges is a persuasive and highly political argument for refocusing the control of food production and consumption within democratic processes rooted in localized food systems.

Now, when there is intense debate about how the world will halve poverty and eradicate hunger, the policies that govern the way food is produced, consumed and distributed, how it is processed and traded, and who controls the food chain, need to be looked at comprehensively. This timely paper points a way forward and invites a more focused consideration of the principles behind what is fast becoming recognized as the most important food and agriculture policy consensus for the 21st century.

Patrick Mulvany
Senior Policy Adviser
ITDG
March 2005

Acknowledgements

The authors would like to express their gratitude to all those who lent their generous support and advice throughout the writing of this paper. First and foremost, to ITDG for commissioning, proof-reading and the lay-out of this paper and, in particular, to Chris Emerson for editing various drafts. Special thanks also go to Patrick Mulvany for his invaluable feedback, constructive comments and great patience.

We would also like specially to thank La Vía Campesina and the IPC, the International NGO/CSO Planning Committee for Food Sovereignty, for the fruitful exchange of ideas that provided important inputs into the present publication.

Finally, a warm thank you as well to all the others who contributed in different ways to this paper.

Michael Windfuhr
Jennie Jonsén

Acronyms

AoA	Agreement on Agriculture (WTO)
CBD	Convention on Biological Diversity (UN)
CESCR	Committee on Economic, Social and Cultural Rights (UN)
CSO	Civil Society Organization
FAO	Food and Agriculture Organization of the United Nations
FDIs	Foreign Direct Investments
FIAN	FoodFirst Information and Action Network
FIVIMS	Food Insecurity and Vulnerability Information Mapping Systems (FAO)
GATS	General Agreement on Trade in Services
GMOs	Genetically Modified Organisms
IATP	Institute for Agriculture and Trade Policy
ICESCR	International Covenant on Economic, Social and Cultural Rights
IFAD	International Fund for Agricultural Development
IFIs	International Financial Institutions
IMF	International Monetary Fund
IPC	International Planning Committee for Food Sovereignty
IPRs	Intellectual Property Rights
ITDG	Intermediate Technology Development Group
ITPGRFA	International Treaty on Plant Genetic Resources for Food and Agriculture (FAO)
MDG	Millennium Development Goal
NGO	Non-governmental Organization
OECD	Organisation for Economic Co-operation and Development
OHCHR	Office of the High Commissioner for Human Rights
PoA	Plan of Action from the 1996 World Food Summit (FAO)
PRSP	Poverty Reduction Strategy Paper
SCM	Agreement on Subsidies and Countervailing Measures (WTO)
SPS	Agreement on Sanitary and Phytosanitary Measures (WTO)
TBT	Technical Barriers to Trade (WTO)
TNCs	Trans-national Corporations
TRIPs	Agreement on Trade-related Aspects of Intellectual Property Rights (WTO)
UDHR	Universal Declaration of Human Rights
UN	United Nations
VG	Voluntary Guidelines [on the right to adequate food]
WANAHR	World Alliance for Nutrition and Human Rights
WFC	World Food Council
WFFS	World Forum on Food Sovereignty
WFS	World Food Summit (FAO, 1996)
WFS:*fyl*	World Food Summit: *five years later* (FAO, 2002)
WSSD	World Summit on Sustainable Development
WTO	World Trade Organization

About the authors

Michael Windfuhr is Secretary General of FIAN-International. He began working for FIAN in 1988, on Latin American issues, and during the 1990s worked at FIAN part-time while co-ordinating a research project on trade and environment at IIASA (International Institute for Applied Systems Analysis) in Laxemburg, Austria (1991), teaching international relations and economic policy at the University of Heidelberg (1993–95), and lecturing at Heidelberg's Institute for Political Science (1995–2000). Michael has published articles in scientific journals and newspapers, and several books on international economics.

Jennie Jonsén is a political scientist, educated at the University of Umeå, Sweden. She works as policy researcher in the International Secretariat of FIAN-International.

About FIAN-International

FIAN-International is a membership-based human rights organisation that focuses on economic, social and cultural rights, particularly on the right to adequate food.

PO Box 10 22 43
D-69012 Heidelberg
Germany
Tel: +49 6221 6530050
Fax: +49 6221 830545
E-mail: windfuhr@fian.org

Executive summary

The development of ideas for the new Food Sovereignty policy framework is progressing rapidly. It has become a focus of interest not only for farmers' organizations, but also for fisherfolk, pastoralists and indigenous peoples' organizations as well as non-governmental organizations (NGOs) and civil society organizations (CSOs). Behind the development of the concept of Food Sovereignty lies a global social network of NGOs, CSOs and social movements and many conferences, forums and declarations. Via Campesina, the global farmers' movement, developed the concept in the early 1990s, with the objective of encouraging NGOs and CSOs to discuss and promote alternatives to neo-liberal policies for achieving food security. Since the concept was launched to the general public at the World Food Summit in 1996 an ever-growing number of NGOs, CSOs and social movements have made policy statements on Food Sovereignty directed at a broad array of institutions. (For a summary of the development of the concept of Food Sovereignty see the appendix.)

The current problems of hunger and malnutrition, as well as rural poverty, have become a priority challenge for international policy. Even though the problems have received some attention at the international level, for example with the adoption of the Rome Declaration of the World Food Summit in 1996 calling for the number of the hungry to be halved by 2015, the incorporation of this in the first Millennium Development Goal, and the overall orientation of some bi- and multilateral aid policies intended to achieve this goal, traditional approaches have failed to address the problems adequately. The latest FAO figures show that the positive trends in the reduction of the number of the hungry and malnourished people that were reported for the first half of the 1990s have reversed: between 1995 and 2005 the number of chronically hungry in developing countries increased at a rate of almost 5 million per year – from 800 million to 852 million.

Food Sovereignty focuses attention on the international 'framework' (World Trade Organization, International Monetary Fund, World Bank, etc.) and the international causes of hunger and malnutrition. It focuses too on national policies that can be oriented towards reducing rural poverty and eliminating hunger and malnutrition. The right to adequate food is a legal reference instrument and provides legal standards for all measures and policies undertaken by each state to secure access to adequate food for everybody. It requires that the framework operates properly and that states implement their obligations under the right to adequate food and other human rights.

Current mainstream answers to the problems causing malnutrition are failing and adherence to a set of central ideas or principles, based around an ever-greater concentration on trade-based food security, is inadequate to tackle the problems. Additional analysis and a search for new, innovative solutions are needed. The World Food Summit Plan of Action contained commitments for nation states, but follow-up has been weak and does not tackle the contradictions between different elements of its action plan.

Strategies to reduce hunger, malnutrition and rural poverty require a new focus on rural development and rural areas. For the next four decades, it is estimated that the majority of the world's poor population will continue to live in rural areas. Food Sovereignty policies are a necessary and important contribution to current debate by concentrating attention on the perspectives of those who face hunger and malnutrition.

This principle is common to all the different interpretations of Food Sovereignty: they start their analyses from the perspective of those facing hunger and rural poverty. The debate on the different instruments and their potential has only relatively recently started among the different civil society actors. It is a dynamic debate that needs further support and enrichment from civil society and scientific contributions, because giving credible and effective answers to the overall problem is not an easy task. The further development of the Food Sovereignty framework would probably be enhanced if it were possible to implement several of the ideas in parallel. Some initiatives have already started, for example some co-ordination of views is being achieved through the IPC for Food Sovereignty in Rome. For the time being, though, the most important outcome could be to enrich the debate and discuss the relevance of different potential policy changes. Each NGO, CSO or social movement should then decide which strategic element it can support.

At present, one cannot distil a fully-fledged 'Food Sovereignty model' in the sense of a ready-made set of policies already available for national and global governance of rural and agricultural policies. Even though many key elements of such a new policy proposal have already been identified and formulated, the overall concept and strategy needs further improvement and clarification, as this paper shows. The use of terminology and definitions, particularly the rights-based language, also needs to be more precise. Several issues have not been addressed properly, such as the situation of the urban poor and their access to food. These are areas in which further debate is needed. The framework has not yet been finalized: it is still being formed.

The purpose of this paper is to show how the Food Sovereignty policy framework has developed and what the basic assumptions and underlying analyses are. It analyses how the framework relates to the current problems in rural and agricultural policies and discusses possible policy constraints to adoption of the Food Sovereignty policy framework. It ends with an encouragement to take the approach seriously and an invitation to join the discussion on the further development of the Food Sovereignty policy framework.

Food Sovereignty is the new policy framework being proposed by social movements all over the world for the governance of food and agriculture, because it addresses the core problems of hunger and poverty in a new and innovative way. It deserves serious consideration.

Introduction

The concept of Food Sovereignty has been developing rapidly since it was first proposed a decade ago. It is becoming a reference point for discourse on food issues, particularly among social movements around the world. It is no longer discussed by farmers' organizations alone, it is also increasingly referred to by pastoralist, fisherfolk, and indigenous peoples' organizations and by associated NGOs and CSOs, and is starting to be recognized by some United Nations' agencies. It is therefore an appropriate time to analyse the different interpretations of and suggestions for implementing the framework in order to understand its potential.

The term 'Food Sovereignty' has been used increasingly since the mid-1990s. It is an umbrella term for particular approaches to tackling the problems of hunger and malnutrition, as well as promoting rural development, environmental integrity and sustainable livelihoods. This approach is being developed and discussed as a counter-proposal to the mainstream development paradigm built on liberalized international agricultural trade, trade-based food security, and industrial agriculture and food production by well-resourced producers. Food Sovereignty has become the new policy framework for challenging current trends in rural development and food and agricultural policies that do not respect or support the interests and needs of smallholder farmers, pastoralists and fisherfolk[1] and the environment.

While there is no universally agreed definition for the term 'Food Sovereignty', an increasing number of documents have offered interpretations. One of the most commonly used is from the People's Food Sovereignty Network (2002):

> *Food Sovereignty is the right of peoples to define their own food and agriculture; to protect and regulate domestic agricultural production and trade in order to achieve sustainable development objectives; to determine the extent to which they want to be self reliant; to restrict the dumping of products in their markets; and to provide local fisheries-based communities the priority in managing the use of and the rights to aquatic resources. Food Sovereignty does not negate trade, but rather it promotes the formulation of trade policies and practices that serve the rights of peoples to food and to safe, healthy and ecologically sustainable production.*

Many NGOs, CSOs and farmers' organizations and their social movements use this definition in their policy documents and have contributed to the development of the framework.

Discussion of Food Sovereignty policies is spreading beyond these organizations and movements. Intergovernmental organizations such as the Food and Agriculture Organization of the United Nations (FAO) have started to investigate the content and scope of the Food Sovereignty policy framework and the first academic articles are now being published. Some political parties have also incorporated it into their agendas (for example the annual P7 Summit in 2001, organized by the Greens/ European Free Alliance, recognized Food Sovereignty as an alternative to existing trade polices).

1

Context: Poverty, hunger and malnutrition

According to FAO figures, more than 850 million people currently face hunger and malnutrition. Some 815 million of them live in economically developing countries, 76% in rural areas (FAO, 2004a, pp.6–10). All available data and studies show that the number of hungry and malnourished people has increased in the last decade, even though enough food is produced globally to satisfy the needs of the world's population. Hunger and malnutrition today are not caused by food shortage, or scarcity: hunger is an issue of *access* to food, to an adequate income, or to productive resources that allow poor people to either produce or buy enough food. The inequitable distribution of food, land, and other productive resources are the main causes of hunger and malnutrition.

The World Food Summit (WFS) in 1996 committed governments to halving the number of hungry people by 2015.[2] This goal was later integrated into the first Millennium Development Goal (MDG) set by the General Assembly of the United Nations in 2000. At the World Food Summit: *five years later* (WFS:*fyl*) in June 2002,[3] it was clear that this goal would not be achieved unless substantial policy changes were made. FAO itself argued in the final declaration that the situation was caused by a 'lack of political will' to implement policies that would reduce hunger and by the lack of investment.[4] NGOs/CSOs and social movements said in the concluding statement of the parallel 'Forum for Food Sovereignty' that not only was the political will to combat hunger lacking but also that at the same time too much political will is used to promote policies that actually exacerbate hunger. It is clear that strategies to overcome or reduce hunger, malnutrition and rural poverty need to both promote new policies as well as challenge the national and international policy environment that hinders access to productive resources or to an income sufficient to feed oneself for so many people worldwide.

Regular reviews of the status of hunger and malnutrition are provided in United Nations reports presented by the Millennium Project. To recommend how to implement the first MDG on poverty and hunger and, specifically, to halve the number of hungry and malnourished people by 2015, a group of experts was set up by the UN Secretary General.[5] This 'Hunger Task Force' developed a typology of the hungry worldwide (see Table 1). Current estimates are that more than 75% of the world's poorest people live in rural areas and depend mainly or partly on agriculture for their livelihoods.

Half the world's hungry people are smallholder farmers who live off a limited area of land, without adequate access to productive resources. Two-thirds of them live on marginal lands in environmentally difficult conditions, such as hillsides or areas threatened by drought or other natural disasters, including flooding, mud slides, etc. They have historically been forced onto marginal lands or have been allowed access to landholdings that are intentionally too small to achieve self-sufficiency. Moreover, 22% of the hungry are landless families, who often survive from income earned under precarious working conditions as labourers. Another 8% are part of the fishing, hunting and herding communities. Secure access to productive resources – land, water, and agricultural inputs such as seeds and livestock breeds, etc. – are therefore key to improving the situation of these families. These inequalities are exacerbated by the fact that the driving force of food and agricultural policies of many countries, in both the industrialized North and the global South, has been industrial agriculture and livestock production and commercial fisheries, and not the needs of smallholder farmers, pastoralists and fisherfolk to have secure access to the productive resources they require. All definitions of Food Sovereignty reflect this challenge and highlight the importance of improving resource access rights as well as equitable trade policies and sustainable production practices, and establishing the Right to Food.

There are still a number of myths and assumptions about why hunger and malnutrition exist in a world of plenty, many of which refer to natural disasters and conflict. Environmental factors such as unreliable rain or storms and drought are often thought to be the main reasons behind famine and hunger, along with complex political situations such as conflicts and civil war. According to the Millennium Project, around 60 million people are currently affected by civil strife and insecure political conditions.

Even though these explanations are indeed relevant, they address the symptoms that occur in situations where people are poor and vulnerable rather than the underlying causes. The reason why poor people are the most affected by natural disasters is due to their lack of reserves, power, and possibilities, and their lack of control over resources.

Table 1 A typology of hunger

Type of household	% of the hungry
Food-producing households in higher-risk environments and remote areas	50
Non-farm rural households	22
Poor urban households	20
Herders, fishers and forest-dependent households	8

Cutting across the above groups:

Vulnerable individuals	Vulnerable pregnant and nursing women and their infants, pre-school children, chronically ill or disabled, several hundred million
Victims of extreme events	About 60 million
HIV-related food insecurity	Number of food-insecure households with adults or children infected by HIV, about 150 million.

Source: UNDP (2003a, p.15)

It is important to note that several authors warn that the current relative overproduction of food, although distribution is inequitable, is a temporarily fortunate situation that may change in the future. There are three sets of opinions about the causes of declining future food availability per capita. Some refer to the expected increase in world population (Population Reference Bureau, 2003). Others highlight the growing demand for food, particularly in successful developing countries, where increasing wealth leads to a changing diet towards more animal products raised on grain.[6] A third set focuses on the anticipated escalation in the degradation of agricultural lands, grazing and fishery resources. Degradation can be caused by urbanization and increased infrastructure, the loss of fertile soils through soil erosion, salinization, contamination, and so on. The availability of irrigation water will decrease, fishing grounds are overexploited and grazing land is often vulnerable to desertification. Additionally, the expected negative impact of climate change must be taken into consideration. (For a good overview of the relationship between climate change and agriculture see FAO (2003b, p.357–72).)

Limitations of technical solutions

The standard answers given concerning these challenges are normally technical. Suggested solutions are often to increase productivity and the yield per hectare through the use of modern plant varieties. This is a typical answer presented by, for example, seed companies and their researchers to justify work on industrial production systems. While it may not be wrong to seek options to improve productivity per area of land, it is becoming increasingly recognized that it is the marginalized communities, rather than the already intensively cultivated agricultural land, that need more attention. Moreover, further intensification in more favourable areas is reaching its limits, for example due to the increasing shortage of water and therefore irrigation possibilities, or through increasing environmental problems, such as salinization, that the current intensive industrialized production is already causing. Jules Pretty argues that it is sustainable and agroecological agriculture involving millions of smallholder farmers across the world that could yield considerable increases and help restore water reserves – it is only industrialized agriculture that has reached the limits of sustainable expansion (Pretty, 2001).

Combating the processes of land degradation and the pressures from population growth are issues that hardly get any support from either national or international policies. Today it is increasingly recognized that those marginalized smallholder farmer groups which have never received sufficient attention or research support could easily increase their yields – often three- or fourfold – in a different policy environment.[7] This potential for increasing yields depends on different factors, such as the type of agricultural system (organic or non-organic), environmental conditions for agriculture, and the respective ecosystems.

Long-term solutions for achieving higher yields, which can be secured sustainably, are the most important. They will require agroecological solutions that will increase productivity on marginal soils, but also convert damaging industrial production systems. Miguel Altieri (2002) noted that, *'Throughout the developing world, resource-poor farmers (about 1.4 billion people) located in risk-prone, marginal environments, remain untouched by modern agricultural technology'.*

Altieri (2002, p.1) states that a new approach to natural resource management must be developed so that new systems can be tailored and adapted in a site-specific way to the highly variable and diverse farm conditions typical of resource-poor farmers. Agroecology provides the scientific basis to address production in a biodiverse agroecosystem able to support itself. The latest advances in agroecological research need to promote natural resource management that is compatible with the needs and aspirations of smallholder farmers. *'Obviously, a relevant research agenda setting should involve the full participation of farmers with other institutions serving a facilitating role. The implementation of the agenda will also imply major institutional and policy changes.'*

Policy constraints

But the problems cannot just be tackled at the technical level. The situation of the rural poor has been aggravated by the fact that rural areas are neglected in national and international policymaking. For a long time the policy focus was on investments in industry and urban infrastructure and budget allocations for rural areas were reduced substantially – often by more than 50% (FAO, 2002a). The same happened with bi- and multilateral aid budgets.[8] Support for rural development and agricultural production was judged as outmoded and has been reduced by more than half since the beginning of the 1990s. Recently international organizations have begun to recognize that the policy shift away from rural development policies was too radical and the policies are now being reversed. A decade of official work on poverty reduction without major results has lead to the realization that policies aiming at effective poverty reduction have to address the needs of people in rural areas (see IFAD, 2001). The FAO is also arguing that the hope of the 1990s, that poverty reduction will automatically lead to a decrease in the number of hungry and malnourished, can no longer be justified. In fact, recognition of the opposite argument – that hunger needs to be tackled first in order to address the problems of poverty – is gaining ground.

In many developing countries agriculture is taxed and support services are poorly equipped. Agricultural research is directed mainly towards commercial crops. But other negative conditions such as insecure land titles and problems of access to resources such as credit or capital, etc. often prevail. The result is that even if smallholders do have access to some land, they have to endure poor conditions, and lack both technical and economic support and adequate economic frameworks. Governments seldom pay enough attention to these sectors and do not fulfil their human rights obligations to these groups.

International policy also has an important impact on marginal rural smallholder farmers' communities and those of pastoralists and fisherfolk. As international polices set binding conditions for national policies, it is the combination of national and international policies that together play a crucial role:

- **Structural adjustment policies have been implemented in most developing countries since the middle of the 1980s.** These policies were built around what the World Bank referred to as the 'trade-based food security' policy package. The World Bank and the International Monetary Fund (IMF) have been influential in urging countries to open up their agricultural markets to cheap imports. Based on the old economic recommendation to produce products in which countries have a comparative advantage, the policy advice has often been to increase imports of 'cheap' staple foods from the world market and exports of commodities such as grains, oil crops and sugar, or to increase production of agricultural export crops in order to finance other imports. The newly developed instruments of the World Bank and the IMF, namely the Poverty Reduction Strategy Papers (PRSPs), which aim to direct policy processes for highly indebted countries, seldom take agriculture and rural development properly on board see SLE, 2002).

- **Trade policies became binding for many countries when the World Trade Organization (WTO) was created in 1995.** The trade rules agreed in the agricultural package (Agreement on Agriculture – AoA) were not significantly different from the policy recommendations given previously by the World Bank and the IMF. The difference was that the rules for trade now became fixed in a binding international agreement which member countries had to obey, since they could otherwise face penalties or sanctions through the dispute settlement procedure. Moreover, trade policy rules are becoming increasingly important since they set not only the terms for tariffs, but also stringent conditions and regulations for national policies. From food safety regulations to intellectual property protection, from agricultural subsidies to price support for basic staple foods, the WTO regulations are deeply affecting national policy frameworks.

Market distortions

One of the bigger problems linked to the WTO AoA is the imbalance in the level of liberalization obligations for different groups of countries. While developing countries have opened up their markets during the last fifteen years, their smallholder farmers still have to compete with subsidized exports from industrialized countries. Because poor countries are not able to pay subsidies to their farmers and are forced to remove trade barriers, almost no agricultural policy instruments prevail in these countries. At the same time industrialized countries are still paying subsidies to their farm sector, even though the bulk of them do not reach small-holder farmers, but rather go to agribusinesses and the grain trading companies. The amount of subsidies provided, particularly export subsidies, enable developed countries to sell their products at lower prices than the cost of production, some-times in both food exporting and importing countries. In fact world market prices are depressed for most staple food products. This forces poor farmers into unfavourable competitive situations. In India, for example, imports of dairy sur-pluses subsidized by the EU have had a negative impact on local, family-based dairy production. Likewise, the export of industrial pork from the US to the Caribbean has destroyed the local Caribbean market.[9] Food aid can also be misused as a form of export subsidy. As a result local smallholder and family farms are dis-appearing as their products are not able to compete on the global market, nor are they able to feed their communities. This can even be found within the EU where, for example, 17,000 farmers and farmworkers left the land in the UK in the 12 months up to June 2003 (FARM, 2004), and currently across the EU one farm is lost every minute.

The liberal response to these market distortions is to liberalize more comprehen-sively. Would a further reduction in subsidy levels in industrialized countries improve the situation for producers in developing countries? Yes it could, but unfortunately not to the extent that would be helpful for many of the marginal-ized smallholder farmers, pastoralists and fisherfolk facing hunger and malnutri-tion. It would be particularly helpful for larger-scale competitive producers in developing countries as they could get better market opportunities, especially for exports, and developing countries might penetrate markets which are currently occupied by developed countries.

Other problems which make it difficult for marginalized producers to make use of the opportunities created by international markets, are:

- **The situation is still far from a reality in which one can expect an end to the existing market distortion.** The current status of the WTO agricultural negotiations shows some progress but it is slow. In the framework agreement reached at the beginning of August 2004 it was agreed that export subsidies should be phased out. No implementation date was agreed, however. At the same time there are only small signs of progress concerning indirect forms of dumping through internal subsidies. Overall support to agriculture in the North remains at the same level as it has been for many years, while the forms of subsidization are becoming a bit less trade distorting. Solutions under dis-cussion may still allow the extensive use of subsidies in the future. Policies of support for poor smallholder farmers in developing countries will therefore need to seriously consider defensive measures in order to respond to these price-distorting subsidies.

- **The opening up of agricultural markets for food imports puts many small and medium producers in developing countries in direct competition with competitors on the world market.** In most of the poorer developing countries, producers with little access to factors of production such as support structures, credit, land and water, or seeds, livestock breeds and fertilizers (particularly smallholder farmers in Africa, mainly women) are often competing with subsi-dized large-scale farmers from industrialized countries. The OECD reports that farmers in industrialized countries do not have natural comparative advan-tages, but often acquire them. Their ability to produce more competitively is grounded in their history of support through subsidies, while smallholder farm-ers in developing countries have often been taxed. As an example, the North

American Free Trade Agreement forces traditional corn producers in Mexico – who normally cultivate 4 hectares of land – to compete with 1,000-hectare subsidized farms in the US.

- **The pressure on prices is fostered by a growing international food processing industry, which has a predominant interest in the cheap supply of inputs.** Commodity trading companies try to out-source internationally at as low a cost as possible. Open market arrangements are therefore favourable for the international food processing industry and less so for local food processing units or farm-based activities. Concentration and internationalization in the food industry is increasing and putting intense pressure on primary producers to produce at a low cost.

Industrialization of agriculture

Furthermore, the industrialization of agriculture has resulted in the consolidation of agricultural land and assets in the hands of big landowners, agribusinesses, and other large commercial entities. Whereas the most fertile and extensive areas of land remain in the hands of a decreasing number of producers, in many countries smallholders are being excluded and forced onto unproductive land. Moreover, reduced resources and increased poverty forces smallholders in many places to cultivate the land more intensively, and to abandon more environmentally sustainable agricultural methods. However, it would be wrong to conclude that it is smallholders that constitute the main threat to the environment. Obviously smallholder farmers, pastoralists and fisherfolk can cause environmental problems such as soil erosion. But at the same time they have been the main custodians of the environment for millennia. The diversity of sustainable uses of land, soil, water, forest, and genetic resources such as seeds and livestock breeds are the result of the careful work and knowledge of many generations of rural and indigenous peoples.

The main environmental threats in global agricultural production come from the industrialization of production, often in more favourable areas. The overuse of water resources, the loss of soil through erosion and salinization, the loss of agricultural biodiversity through the simplification of production and the destruction of agroecosystems, intensive animal production, and over-fishing are all results of the open world market and the low prices for all major commodities, which piles on enormous pressure to produce as cheaply as possible.[10]

Corporate control

Large-scale industrial trans-national corporations (TNCs) are also exerting increased control over different parts of the food system, its markets, and worldwide food production.[11] The input sectors of the food production industry is undergoing rapid concentration. Many traditional seed-producing companies have been bought by agrochemical companies or oil-companies. Intellectual property rights (IPR) systems are promoted that provide monopoly privileges over what was once common property and thus facilitate the control over genetic material and life forms such as seeds and livestock breeds. These systems not only prevent the free exchange of these seeds and livestock breeds, but also allow corporations to expropriate farmers' knowledge of food production and prevent farmers from sharing this.

Today TNCs own whole sequences of genes in, for example, soya. This means that they are able to control more and more of the production cycle and force farmers to buy licenses in order to continue farming. Intellectual property rights agreements are another obstacle to the spread of knowledge and technology among smallholder farmers and to their access to seeds and livestock breeds. The WTO's Agreement on Trade Related Aspects of Intellectual Property Rights (TRIPs) requires all members of the WTO to implement plant variety protection legislation, through patents or other IPR systems, at the same level as the most developed countries. Historically a nation's patent legislation system is gradually implemented in line with the country's industrialization and development of science and technology. The fact that developing counties lack the resources to establish a patent system as advanced as the rich counties is clearly reflected in the distribution of the patent applications on plant and animal resources. Whereas more than 90% of genetic resources for food and agriculture are from biotopes in the South, corporations in developed countries claim 98% of the patents on genes and living organisms.

This process of concentration is also visible in other input sectors for agriculture, such as the production of pesticides, as well as in the food trade and the food processing industry. All global transactions in cereals and soybeans are controlled by a few companies. The same is true for other important international crops, such as tropical export crops like bananas, pineapples, coffee, cocoa, etc. The strongest pressure on prices comes from international food processing industries (see, for example, UK Food Group, 2003).

In reality it is not just at the input end of agriculture that corporate dominance prevails. Over the last two decades TNCs have increased their market domination of the processing and retailing of food. Smallholder farmers who are able to produce enough to trade are now facing an ever-harder struggle to exert any influence not only over the farm inputs they need, but also over the farmgate price for their produce and the terms and conditions of its trade (see Christian Aid, 2003). New approaches that empower farmers and re-localize food systems are needed. In Europe, where the TNC dominance of food retailing has been an issue for some time, there are already a number of farmer-based initiatives including farmers' markets, Fairtrade, farm retail outlets and vegetable box schemes that help to 'localize' food systems and empower smallholder farmers (see, for example, Sustain, 2003).

Conclusion

In conclusion, people facing hunger and malnutrition are, to a large extent, smallholders, landless workers, pastoralists or fisherfolk, often situated in marginal and vulnerable ecological environments. Moreover, they are often neglected by both national and international policies. Without proper support they cannot compete with increasingly subsidized industrialized agriculture. For many of them market liberalization has resulted in damaging and often unfair competition with farmers or commercial entities that have 'acquired' comparative advantages through decades of direct and indirect subsidies. The situation often results in smallholders being forced off their land and moving to even more marginal areas or migrating to the shantytowns around cities.

Without addressing the structural causes of poverty, hunger and malnutrition, a fruitful and thorough discussion about how to reduce poverty cannot be undertaken. In meeting these challenges it will be necessary to address these causes, most of which are directly related to a system where local development, social and environmental goals – particularly with respect to marginalized smallholder farmers, pastoralists and fisherfolk – are not adequately taken into consideration. For the majority of the rural poor, changes are needed, to end the failure of national and international policies to increase the ability of countries and communities to define their own agricultural, pastoral, fisheries, and food polices which are ecologically, socially, economically and culturally appropriate to their circumstances. These are key areas for policy reform.

2
Core elements of Food Sovereignty

Behind the development of the Food Sovereignty framework policy lies a global network of non-governmental and civil society organizations and social movements, and a number of conferences, forums and declarations which have resulted in several significant statements on 'Food Sovereignty' (see the appendix for a detailed history of the use of the term).

The Food Sovereignty policy framework includes a set of principles that protect the policy space for peoples and countries to define their agricultural and food policies, and their models of production and food consumption patterns. For many groups the right to produce and the right to food are mutually linked since most of the hungry and malnourished in the world are smallholders and landless farmers. During the World Food Summit, Via Campesina presented a set of requirements that would offer an alternative to the world trade policies and realize the human right to food. In the statement, 'Food Sovereignty: A Future without Hunger' (1996), it declared that *'Food Sovereignty is a precondition to genuine food security'*, and the right to food can therefore be seen as the tool to achieve it.

From this initial platform two more concrete policy proposals were launched by the NGOs/CSOs and social movements during the World Food Summit in 1996. In the final document of the parallel forum, 'Profit for few or food for all', civil society organizations demanded the development of two new international legal instruments:

1. *A Code of Conduct on the Right to Adequate Food; and*

2. *A Global Convention on Food Security.*[12]

While the first instrument has been followed up since 1996, the second was ignored for several years. Since 2001, however, a number of important events have taken place in which the Food Sovereignty policy framework was discussed and developed further.

The discussion about a Global Convention was revitalized in Havana in September 2001, where it was discussed under the term 'Food Sovereignty' rather than food security. This resulted from discussions during the World Social Forum at Porto Alegre, in January 2001, where the organization of a World Forum on Food Sovereignty (WFFS) was agreed for September 2001, a project on which many organizations across the world had been working for a long time. This Forum was held over one week in Cuba and brought together nearly 400 people representing some 60 countries and more than 200 organizations. The Cuban National Association of Small Farmers convened the Forum along with a group of international movements, networks, organizations and people committed to smallholder farmers and indigenous agriculture, pastoralism, artisanal fisheries, sustainable food systems and the peoples' right to feed themselves. Their statements were gathered in the 'Final Declaration of the World Forum on Food Sovereignty'. (See the 'Literature and references' section of this paper for details of where to find all these texts.)

In August 2002 the Asian Regional Consultation of NGOs/CSOs gathered in Bangkok, Thailand. The meeting resulted in the statement 'End hunger! Fight for the right to live!', signed by over 80 NGOs from 14 Asian countries.

Parallel to the WFS:*fyl*, in Rome, 2002, the second Forum for Food Sovereignty was held, representing some 700 NGOs, CSOs and social movements. This parallel forum was co-ordinated by an International NGO/CSO Planning Committee (IPC).[13] As a result of the parallel forum the statement, 'Food Sovereignty: A right for all', was published (NGO/CSO Forum for Food Sovereignty, 2002). The campaign for Food Sovereignty continued at the World Summit for Sustainable Development in the end of August in the same year.

In November 2002, the 'International Forum on Food Sovereignty and an Agro-Ecological Fair' took place in Bucaramanga, Colombia, organized by, among others, Friends of the Earth, Colombia.

For the WTO meeting in Cancun in September 2003, another statement, 'Our world is not for sale. Priority to Peoples' Food Sovereignty. WTO out of Food and Agriculture' was written by the People's Food Sovereignty Network. This network is a loose global coalition of smallholder farmer organizations and NGOs working on food and agriculture issues and to a great extent it consists of the same organizations as the IPC.

In 2004 Asian NGOs, CSOs and social movements organized the People's Caravan for Food Sovereignty that travelled through 13 countries across South Asia, South-East Asia, East Asia and three countries in Europe. and culminated in a week of events in Nepal with the Prime Minister of Nepal, Mr Sher Bahadur Deuba, inaugurating the final event.

When it comes to trade policy objectives to achieve Food Sovereignty, NGOs, CSOs and social movements have been remarkably united in their approach. Considering the statements and declarations as well as the additional literature presented, it is indeed possible to outline a framework of policies that have broad support. Even though NGOs, CSOs and social movements agree on the overall framework of policies to achieve Food Sovereignty, however different groups have emphasized different issues within this framework. The policy framework to achieve Food Sovereignty is indeed highly comprehensive and flexible. For many groups the right to produce and the right to food are mutually linked since most of the hungry and malnourished in the world are smallholders and landless farmers. The definition based on these considerations that was made by the IPC in 2002 was:

'Food Sovereignty is the Right of peoples, communities, and countries to define their own agricultural, labour, fishing, food and land policies, which are ecologically, socially, economically and culturally appropriate to their unique circumstances. It includes the true right to food and to produce food, which means that all people have the right to safe, nutritious and cultural appropriate food and to food-producing resources and the ability to sustain themselves and their societies.'[14]

The text was later amended in a meeting of the IPC in October 2004 to correct the original text. The first sentence now reads: 'Food Sovereignty is the right of individuals, communities, peoples and countries to define. . .' The amendment of the text to include 'individuals' was made to highlight that the right to food that is recognized in the second sentence is a human right, which is also an individual right. The individual right component was not excluded by intention. This amendment will overcome the criticism by human rights groups of the original formulation, which could have been read as not incorporating the right to adequate food of the individual. The clarification is helpful to highlight the relationship between the right to food and Food Sovereignty.

The change made in October 2004 was already taken up by the Asian civil society that published a draft of a 'Peoples' Convention on Food Sovereignty' that was released in July 2004.[15] The second paragraph of the preamble says:

> *'By this Convention, Food Sovereignty becomes the right of people and communities to decide and implement their agricultural and food policies and strategies for sustainable production and distribution of food. It is the right to adequate, safe, nutritional and culturally appropriate food and to produce food sustainably and ecologically. It is the right to access of productive resources such as land, water, seeds and biodiversity for sustainable utilization.'*

This text reflects that the right to food as a fundamental human right is also an individual right, given claims for respect of human dignity by the nation state. Still the text merges rights that are already recognized in binding international law such as the right to adequate food, with rights that so far do not exist formally, such as the 'right to produce food sustainably and ecologically'. The second use of the rights language is a political one. The two levels of rights language must be differentiated in order not to lower the standards of recognition that the right to adequate food has already reached in international law.

Between the definitions presented here, one can find only marginal differences. However, the IPC definition incorporates even more elements than the former Via Campesina definition, which shows that the framework is becoming more comprehensive. Most definitions of Food Sovereignty now include the following elements:

- priority of local agricultural production to feed people locally;

- access of smallholder farmers, pastoralists, fisherfolk and landless people to land, water, seeds and livestock breeds and credit. Hence the need for land reform; for the fight against GMOs and patents on seeds, livestock breeds and genes; for free access to seeds and livestock breeds by smallholder farmers and pastoralists and for safeguarding water as a public good to be distributed equitably and sustainably used; and for secure access to fishing grounds by artisanal fisherfolk;

- the right to food;

- the right of smallholder farmers to produce food and a recognition of Farmers Rights;

- the right of consumers to decide what they consume, and how and by whom it is produced;

- the right of countries to protect themselves from under-priced agricultural and food imports;

- the need for agricultural prices to be linked to production costs and to stop all forms of dumping. Countries or unions of states are entitled to impose taxes on excessively cheap imports, if they commit themselves to using sustainable production methods and if they control production in their internal markets to avoid structural surpluses (supply management);

- the populations' participation in agricultural policy decision-making;

- the recognition of the rights of women farmers who play a major role in agricultural production in general and in food production in particular;

- agroecology as a way not only to produce food but also to achieve sustainable livelihoods, living landscapes and environmental integrity.

While this set of elements can be found in nearly all definitions of Food Sovereignty the specific combination of factors as well as the actual focus vary in different definitions. The Forum on Food Sovereignty in 2002 debated the elements of Food Sovereignty and subsequently these were summarised by the IPC for Food Sovereignty into four priority areas for action:

1. **Right to Food**
   To promote the adoption of a rights-based approach to food and agricultural policies that will lead to an end to violations of the right to adequate food and will reduce, and progressively eliminate, hunger and malnutrition, which is now recognized as an individual's right.

   The right to adequate food is foremost a right of each person to safe, nutritious and culturally acceptable food. To fully implement the right to adequate food all people need to have physical and economic access to sufficient quantities of safe, nutritious, and culturally appropriate food and food-producing resources, including access to land, water, and seeds.

2. **Access to Productive Resources**
   To promote continued access of smallholder farmers, pastoralists, fisherfolk and indigenous peoples to, and the equitable sharing of benefits from, the sustainable use of their land, waters, genetic and other natural resources used for food and agricultural production. A genuine agrarian reform is necessary which gives landless and farming people – especially women – ownership and control of the land they work and returns territories to indigenous peoples.

   In the case of genetic resources, this access is seen by civil society organizations as continued access unrestricted by intellectual property rights to seeds and livestock breeds and wider agricultural biodiversity; and that the integrity of these genetic resources is not compromised by the spread of GMOs and genetic engineering technologies.

3. **Mainstream Agroecological Production**
   To promote family and community-based agroecological models of food production, in practice and through policy, research and development, in order to help ensure peoples' food security, especially those who are vulnerable to hunger and malnutrition, through the sustainable management of local agroecosystems to produce food for predominately local markets.

   Altieri (1995) defines agroecology as: '. . .the application of ecological concepts and principles to the design and management of sustainable agroecosystems. . .' and continues '. . .agroecology. . . is the discipline that provides the basic ecological principles for how to study, design and manage agroecosystems that are both productive and natural resource conserving, and that are also culturally sensitive, socially just and economically viable. Agroecology goes beyond a one-dimensional view of agroecosystems to embrace an understanding of ecological and social levels of co-evolution, structure and function. . . Agroecology is the holistic study of agroecosystems, including all environmental and human elements.'

   The agroecological approach to agricultural production is increasingly recognized and promoted among NGOs and CSOs as an effective response to the pressing need for food and livelihood security, mainly but not exclusively, for family and community farmers worldwide and especially those living in complex, diverse and risk-prone environments with limited available resources. Several comprehensive studies have been published in recent years (Pretty and Koohafkan, 2002; Scialabba and Hattam, 2002, pp.135 and 144; FAO, 2002b). A study published by the FAO and others before the World Summit in Sus-

tainable Development (WSSD) in Johannesburg in 2002 reports yield increases averaging 94% with best results attaining 600% (Pretty and Koohafkan, 2002).

4. Trade and Local Markets
To promote equitable trade policies which enable communities and countries vulnerable to hunger and malnutrition to produce sufficient quantities of safe and secure food supplies and which militate against the negative effects of subsidized exports, food dumping, artificially low prices and other similar elements characterizing the current model of agricultural trade.

The above four priority areas for action are broadly subscribed to by all proponents of Food Sovereignty and are often referred to as the four 'pillars' or 'principles' of Food Sovereignty. Differences of interpretation appear when it comes to the measures needed to implement or realize the principles and achieve Food Sovereignty. The opinion of many NGOs, CSOs and Social Movements has been that all issues related to the agriculture and food needs of the majority should be removed from the WTO and that new governance processes outside the current trading system should be developed. Some, for example the US National Farmers Union, call for a separate treaty altogether.

Although such differences of interpretation exist, discussions relating to the Food Sovereignty policy framework within civil society are converging. This is not surprising, as the concept of Food Sovereignty emanated from a political discourse focusing on the self-determination of local communities and allowing self-defined ways to seek solutions to local problems. While food security is more of a technical concept, and the right to food a legal one, Food Sovereignty is essentially a political concept. Even though Food Sovereignty has gained some recognition outside civil society groups and social movements, and the policies to achieve it have become more clearly defined, the question remains how advocates of Food Sovereignty could elaborate proposals that would achieve it. The comprehensive nature of the concept of Food Sovereignty implies that a strategy to achieve it will have to be highly complex.

Out of the statements and declarations that have developed over time, it is possible to distinguish at least six concrete policy proposals to achieve Food Sovereignty. (The potential relationships between the different instruments will be discussed in following sections of this paper.)

- A *Code of Conduct on the human Right to Food* to govern the activities of those involved in achieving the right to food, including national and international institutions as well as private actors, such as transnational corporations. Since the World Food Summit:*five years later* the FAO and its members have developed a set of voluntary guidelines for the progressive realization of the right to adequate food. Civil society pressure to adopt a code of conduct was influential in getting work started on voluntary guidelines in 2003. The voluntary guidelines were finally adopted by the FAO-Council in November, 2004. (The text of the guidelines can be found on the FAO website (FAO, 2004b); civil society comments on the guidelines can be found on the FIAN-International website, www.fian.org.)

- An *International Convention on Food Sovereignty* that replaces the current Agreement on Agriculture (AoA) and relevant clauses from other WTO agreements. These include TRIPs, the General Agreement on Trade in Services (GATS), the Agreement on Sanitary and Phytosanitary Measures (SPS), Technical Barriers to Trade (TBT), and the Agreement on Subsidies and Countervailing Measures (SCM). It would implement, within the international policy framework, Food Sovereignty and the basic human rights of all peoples to safe and healthy food, decent and full rural employment, labour rights and protection, and a healthy, rich and diverse natural environment. It would also incorporate trade rules on food and agricultural commodities. Such a convention has been affirmed by several conferences, for example in Thailand in October, 2003 and in the 'Draft Peoples' Convention on Food Sovereignty', in July, 2004.

- A *World Commission on Sustainable Agriculture and Food Sovereignty* established to undertake a comprehensive assessment of the impacts of trade liberalization on Food Sovereignty and security, and develop proposals for change. These would include the agreements and rules within the WTO and other regional and international trade regimes, and the economic policies promoted by international financial institutions (IFIs) and multilateral development banks. Such a commission could be made up of and directed by representatives from various social and cultural groups, peoples' movements, professional institutions, democratically elected representatives and appropriate multilateral institutions.

- A *reformed and strengthened United Nations* (UN), active and committed to protecting the fundamental rights of all peoples, as being the appropriate forum to develop and negotiate rules for sustainable production and fair trade. Several major conventions and treaties have been developed by the United Nations or their subsidiary bodies, such as the International Treaty on Plant Genetic Resources for Food and Agriculture, developed under the FAO in harmony with the Convention on Biological Diversity.

- An *independent dispute settlement mechanism* integrated within an International Court of Justice, especially to prevent dumping and, for example, GMOs in food aid.

- An international, legally binding *treaty* that defines the rights of smallholder farmers to the assets, resources, and legal protections they need to be able to exercise their right to produce. Such a treaty could be framed within the UN Human Rights framework, and be linked to already existing relevant UN conventions. La Via Campesina is currently discussing the idea to demand the development of an 'International Peasant Rights Convention'. A first draft has been developed by the peasant organizations from Indonesia, which is currently being discussed worldwide in the Via Campesina network.

All proposals would require far-reaching changes in the current regulation of international agricultural and trade policies, as the scope of major international institutions and treaties would have to be changed. Food Sovereignty is less a proposal for a single policy change in one of the international regimes, more a framework to change the broad range of agricultural policies worldwide. Under the umbrella of the Food Sovereignty, several new institutional frameworks are possible. Moreover, it is not surprising that NGOs, CSOs and social movements' positions still vary tremendously, since it is not an easy task to develop a new blueprint of institutions and conventions. Via Campesina described seven principles of Food Sovereignty: Food as a Basic Human Right; Agrarian Reform; Protecting Natural Resources; Reorganizing Food Trade; Ending the Globalization of Hunger; Social Peace; and Democratic control (see summary in Box 1 and full text in the appendix on pp 45, 46). Also, the four pillars of Food Sovereignty already described further summarize these issues.

Box 1. Summary of Via Campesina's 'Seven Principles to Achieve Food Sovereignty'

1. **Food: A Basic Human Right** – Everyone must have access to safe, nutritious and culturally appropriate food in sufficient quantity and quality to sustain a healthy life with full human dignity. Each nation should declare that access to food is a constitutional right and guarantee the development of the primary sector to ensure the concrete realization of this fundamental right.

2. **Agrarian Reform** – A genuine agrarian reform is necessary which gives landless and farming people – especially women – ownership and control of the land they work and returns territories to indigenous peoples. The right to land must be free of discrimination on the basis of gender, religion, race, social class or ideology; the land belongs to those who work it.

3. **Protecting Natural Resources** – Food Sovereignty entails the sustainable care and use of natural resources, especially land, water, and seeds and livestock breeds. The people who work the land must have the right to practice sustainable management of natural resources and to conserve biodiversity free of restrictive intellectual property rights. This can only be done from a sound economic basis with security of tenure, healthy soils and reduced use of agro-chemicals.

4. **Reorganizing Food Trade** – Food is first and foremost a source of nutrition and only secondarily an item of trade. National agricultural policies must prioritize production for domestic consumption and food self-sufficiency. Food imports must not displace local production nor depress prices.

5. **Ending the Globalization of Hunger** – Food Sovereignty is undermined by multilateral institutions and by speculative capital. The growing control of multinational corporations over agricultural policies has been facilitated by the economic policies of multilateral organizations such as the WTO, World Bank and the IMF. Regulation and taxation of speculative capital and a strictly enforced Code of Conduct for TNCs is therefore needed.

6. **Social Peace** – Everyone has the right to be free from violence. Food must not be used as a weapon. Increasing levels of poverty and marginalization in the countryside, along with the growing oppression of ethnic minorities and indigenous populations, aggravate situations of injustice and hopelessness. The ongoing displacement, forced urbanization, repression and increasing incidence of racism of smallholder farmers cannot be tolerated.

7. **Democratic control** – Smallholder farmers must have direct input into formulating agricultural policies at all levels. The United Nations and related organizations will have to undergo a process of democratization to enable this to become a reality. Everyone has the right to honest, accurate information and open and democratic decision-making. These rights form the basis of good governance, accountability and equal participation in economic, political and social life, free from all forms of discrimination. Rural women, in particular, must be granted direct and active decision-making on food and rural issues.

3

Comparison of Food Sovereignty with food security and the Right to Food

Apart from Food Sovereignty, two other terms have been used in the discourse on the issue of persistent hunger and malnutrition and in the design of strategies for its eradication: the *right to adequate food* and *food security*. It is important to clarify whether the three terms represent different views of, and approaches to, the fight against hunger, or whether they could be seen as complementary ways of describing and searching for solutions to hunger. A careful definition of each term is required to understand whether, and how, the three policies could be used in a complementary manner, or if they reflect contradictory analyses of the same problems.

Right to Food

The oldest policy is the 'Right to Food', which was recognized in the Universal Declaration of Human Rights in 1948. It is also included in the International Covenant on Economic, Social and Cultural Rights of 1976.[16] The right to food is, therefore, an integral component of human rights. Since it is in the category of a human right rather than being a political concept, it has a different character to food security and Food Sovereignty. All three policies were discussed at the NGO/CSO and social movements' parallel events to the 1996 WFS and to the WFS:*fyl* in 2002.

As a human right, it implies that an individual can require the state and the communities of states to respect, protect and fulfil their needs for appropriate access to sufficient food of an acceptable quality. The right to food provides for individual entitlements and related state obligations, which are to be enshrined in national and international law.[17] In that sense the right to food empowers oppressed communities and individuals against the state and other powerful actors. The normative content was described by the UN Committee on Economic, Social and Cultural Rights (CESCR) in its 'General Comment No.12' (GC 12), as a follow up to the 'World Food Summit Plan of Action' that was demanding such a clarification from member states. In GC 12 the right to adequate food is described as 'the right of every man, woman and child alone and in community with others to have physical and economic access at all times to adequate food or means for its procurement in ways consistent with human dignity'. The definition used in GC 12 also highlights the requirement to ensure access to an income base for each individual either through access to productive resources (land, water, seeds, livestock breeds, fish stocks, etc.) or through work, or, if neither of these is possible, through AN adequate social safety nets. Each of these terms is described in more detail in the text of GC 12. Not only must the food to which access is made possible be sufficient in quantity, but the form of access itself has to have certain qualities: access must be possible by participating in economic life using resources and other means of procurement. Moreover, this form of access must be sustainable.

The state has to *respect, protect* and *fulfil* this standard for each person in its jurisdiction. The crucial issue then is to determine the related state obligations to make sure that laws and programmes exist through which people can make their entitlement a reality. The obligations are best explained in GC 12.[18]

> '*The right to adequate food, like any other human right, imposes three types or levels of obligations on state parties: the obligations to respect, protect and to fulfil. . . The obligations to respect, as existing access to adequate food requires that state parties do not take any measure resulting in preventing such access. The obligation to protect requires measures by the state to ensure that enterprises or individuals do not deprive [other] individuals of their access to adequate food. The obligation to fulfil (facilitate) means that states must pro-actively engage in activities with the intention to strengthen people's access to, and utilisation of, resources and means to ensure their livelihood, including food security. Finally, whenever an individual or group is unable to enjoy the right to adequate food by the means at their disposal, states have the obligation to fulfil (provide) that right directly.*'

State parties also have external obligations with respect to individuals or groups living in other countries.

While the principal obligation under Article 2 of the Covenant is to take steps to achieve the full realization of the right to adequate food, GC 12 clarifies that (a) each state has the 'obligation to proceed as expeditiously as possible towards that goal', and (b) 'every state is obliged to ensure for everyone under its jurisdiction access to the minimum essential food, . . . to ensure their freedom from hunger'. While only states are parties to the Covenant and are thus ultimately accountable for compliance with it, all members of society – individuals, families, local communities, non-governmental organizations, and civil society organizations, as well as the private sector – have responsibilities in the realization of the right to adequate food. The state should provide an environment that facilitates implementation of these responsibilities.

The work of setting the standards of interpretation of the right to food has been promoted by NGOs such as FoodFirst Information Action Network (FIAN) since the Vienna Conference on Human Rights in 1993. In 1996, delegates to the first World Food Summit already showed an interest in promoting the issue of the right to food inside FAO. Since then, the Office of the High Commissioner for Human Rights (OHCHR) has held three expert consultations on the right to food, in 1997, 1998 and 2001, (one of which was co-hosted by the FAO). The results from these consultations have influenced the development of GC 12. GC 12 was also influenced by the parallel NGO/CSO process, which began during the parallel NGO forum to the WFS in 1996. In their final declaration 'Profit for Few or Food for All' the NGOs/CSOs demanded the development of a Code of Conduct on the right to adequate food. The drafting of this code was carried out by FIAN-International, the Institute Jacques Maritain, and World Alliance for Nutrition and Human Rights (WANAHR) in September, 1997. Other advances include the work of the UN Special Rapporteur on the Right to Food, who was appointed by the UN Commission on Human Rights in 2000, as well as various publications on the right to food produced by FAO. In the words of Pierre Spitz (2002), '*these advances are spectacular compared to the development of FAO's follow-up in other areas of the plan of action from the WFS*'.

The standard in interpretation of the right to adequate food that was achieved by GC 12 and was recently supported unanimously in most elements by FAO members. In November, 2004 the FAO council adopted the 'Voluntary guidelines for the progressive realization of the right to adequate food in the context of national food security'. These voluntary guidelines (VG) have been developed following a decision of the World Food Summit: *five years later* to do so. The decision was influenced by pressure from civil society organizations present at the parallel NGO/CSO forum in June, 2002. The text agreed in the negotiating process adopts the standards of interpretation of the right to food that were developed during recent years in the human rights system of the United Nations. While the political commitment to implement the voluntary guidelines is quite weak in several formulations, the VG have achieved a breakthrough in setting standards. Issues such as access to land and water, safety nets, standards for the use of food aid, the prohibition against using food as a weapon in conflicts, etc., are clearly spelt out. The text could become a useful tool for civil society actors to challenge unwilling governments. The VG also addresses the responsibilities governments have concerning international impacts of their own policies.

The right to adequate food has the advantage that it is based on existing international law. The International Covenant on Economic, Social and Cultural Rights is part of the International Bill of Human Rights, and therefore at the core of international law. At the Vienna Conference on Human Rights (1993) states agreed on the 'primacy of human rights obligations' above all other obligations in international law. It can therefore be a strong tool in defending oppressed communities and deprived groups and individuals. When it comes to economic, social and cultural rights, the current weaknesses emanate from the fact that judges and courts in many countries still do not know enough about these rights. It is therefore only recently that the right to food has begun to be used in court proceedings.[19] The definition prepared by the UN Committee on Economic, Social and Cultural Rights, in GC 12, has already gained a lot of support from NGOs and CSOs, academia and by many governments. Now with the Voluntary Guidelines most of the norms of the GC 12 are formally accepted by FAO Members. Using the Voluntary Guidelines now provides a new tool in the defence of the Right to Food that civil society organizations can use in the coming years.

Food security

Food security is the most frequently used term of the three. Since the end of the 1970s, when the term began to be used on a regular basis, it has been reformulated many times. For a long period there were as many definitions as users. The current definition, agreed during the 1996 World Food Summit, is a broad one: *'Food security exists when all people, at all times, have physical and economic access to safe and nutritious food which meets their dietary needs and food preferences for an active and healthy life'*. This is both the vision and the definition of food security used in the 'World Food Summit Plan of Action' and on which the FAO-co-ordinated 'Food insecurity and vulnerability information mapping systems – FIVIMS' are based.[20] However, food security is largely a definition of a goal rather than a programme with specific policies. The implementation strategies required to achieve food security may need to change over time, to address new threats or barriers to achieving food security.

The term food security was developed in the context of the UN-specialized agencies dealing with food and nutrition (see FAO, 1983a). It was then argued that all countries with difficulties in national food supply should 'potentially' have sufficient access to basic food imports. Besides questions of trade policy, such as the access by food-deficient countries to surplus products, the question of the worldwide availability of surplus products and the storage of food reserves were discussed under the umbrella of global food security. Early on it became clear that in order to secure enough food supplies, measures at the national level were also necessary. The 'FAO Plan of Action for World Food Security' adopted in 1979 by the Conference of the FAO, therefore introduced the term *national food security*, which was used to describe ways of achieving a better national distribution of food. Within the framework of 'national food security' aspects such as grain reserves, import and export quotas, food aid, agricultural techniques to increase production, and irrigation were discussed. These notions of food security were, at that time, concentrating on the availability of enough food supplies in national markets and based on population/food availability ratios, and lead strategically to policies for increasing production.

Soon, it was questioned whether these production-oriented policies helped to solve the problems of hunger and malnutrition. Amartya Sen's (1981) seminal work on *Poverty and Famines.* brought considerable challenges to the debate by highlighting the entitlements of individuals and groups to access food. The debate changed gradually from the overall availability of food to the individual's access (entitlement) to food. At the eight-minister meeting of the World Food Council (WFC) in 1982 the decision, under the title 'Food security for people', was passed. In 1983 the Council of the FAO and the WFC followed up with the recommendation for a further definition of food security to include the *access of the individual to food* (WFC, 1983; FAO, 1983b). Since then, the concept of first *household* and later *individual food security* has been developed. (The definition during the middle of the 1980s was 'access by people at all times to enough food for an active and healthy life' (used by FAO and by the World Bank in 1986) (see Eide, A., et al., 1991, pp.416–67).) Throughout the years the scope of Food Security has become increasingly comprehensive. In academic literature the determinants of food security are described in a very similar way as the definition of the right to food. Haddad and Gillespie (2001) describe Food Security with the following determinants: 'Physical access at national level, physical access at local level, economic access, social access, food quality and safety, physiological access, risk of loss of access'.

While such a modern definition of food security focuses predominantly on the individual's access to food, it does still encompass *access to food* in general and *the purchasing of food*. Both right to food and Food Sovereignty debates concentrate instead on *access to productive resources*. The Food Sovereignty framework specifically includes access and control of resources to produce food. Food security, nevertheless, became the central concept used in the intergovernmental process at the World Food Summit as well as in the follow-up process, as the title of the WFS declaration – 'Rome Declaration on World Food Security' – shows. The WFS 'Plan of Action' from 1996 reflected all stages of the food security definition and deals with problems of global, national, household and individual food security.

There are, however, fundamental differences in the language of food security compared to the language of rights:

1. Food security implies a desirable state of affairs which governments claim to work for – however there exists no legally binding state obligations or legal mechanisms linked to it which could be used by the malnourished to defend themselves against the destruction of their access to food by landlords, corporations, state authorities, etc. Under this policy, states cannot be held accountable for being (co)responsible for the situation of hunger and malnutrition of their people.

2. Along with the discussion on household or individual food security, a highly aggregated vision of food security as a global, national or regional issue tends to prevail. Hence the bias towards global, national or regional availability of food, rather than individual access to food by deprived persons or groups. The FIVIMS analysis is becoming more comprehensive in that respect, allowing an improved recognition of typical groups of affected people at the national or regional level. There is, however, still a significant difference between this and a rights-based approach that starts from the entitlement of an individual, family or group.

3. The use of the term food security in many documents misses a crucial element of the right to food. Not only is it important to focus attention on the amount of food people are able to access, but *how* people access this food. The rights-based debate focuses on forms of access that respect human dignity. For the right to food, economic access means much more than adequate purchasing power to buy food. It means access to resources to feed oneself: to land, to seeds and livestock breeds, to water and fishery resources, to basic capital and credit, to skills, etc., which are needed to produce food or to gain an income with dignity.

After decades of discussions about the term 'food security' there is now a list of carefully developed proposals in the '1996 WFS Plan of Action' which governments can use to design effective policies against hunger and malnutrition. It demonstrates that many good proposals for sound policies are available. The food security debate is, therefore, helpful as a tool to discuss the use of certain policy choices. However, the term 'food security' has two important limitations in addition to the elements described above. First, it does not set any priorities when it comes to the implementation of policies. Second, a document such as the 'WFS Plan of Action' contains contradictory recommendations and, so far, there has been no room to discuss the potential conflicts between the recommendations.[21]

Whereas it seems as if the concept of food security is understood today more and more in terms of household or individual food security, the concept does improve the way in which key problems of hunger and malnutrition are addressed. However, as shown for example in the *UNDP Human Development Report 2000*, the original meaning of food security in terms of general food availability at the global and national level is still the norm for most international agencies. As indicators for food security, *HDR 2000* uses data on the national averages of supplies of food energy, protein and fat, the food production index, food imports and food aid. Despite agencies' good intentions, the process of widening and changing mainstream understanding of the concept seems to be lengthy and difficult. The debate inside FAO and the UN food agencies, however, is becoming increasingly oriented towards the 'access dimension', particularly through the FIVIMS work. We have yet to see which interpretation will become more politically powerful. Still, many important opinion formers prefer to focus on global and national availability of food, including, in particular, those who use these data to promote the use of new (industrial) agricultural technologies for increasing yields and productivity.

Comparison

Food security is largely a definition of a goal and is therefore a term that has been interpreted the most broadly. A definition of a goal does not automatically recommend a specific programme to achieve that goal. The Right to Food is similarly a concept that does not rest on a particular set of policies, but focuses on the obligations of states and on allowing people who are negatively affected to use legal remedies to get their rights implemented. States have to guarantee the Right to Food but have a wide margin of discretion on how to implement it. Food Sovereignty, however, is a more precise policy proposal, with proponents challenging political inactivity or other failures to pursue appropriate policies (see, for example, People's Food Sovereignty, 2002). Therefore, the scope of the three terms is not strictly comparable because of their different natures. What can be compared and contrasted are the political consequences that could ensue from the implementation of the different concepts developed to date.

Both the Right to adequate Food and Food Security emphasize the economic access of individuals or households to food. The Right to Food additionally focuses on the economic access to income- or food-producing resources. Moreover, the value added by the rights-based approach is that it addresses obligations and responsibilities of all duty bearers. This gives individuals and groups a claim vis-à-vis the state and states acting together to respect, protect and fulfil their access to adequate food.

The Food Sovereignty framework also applies a rights-based approach. It includes the aspect of the rights of access of smallholder farmers, pastoralists and fisherfolk to food-producing resources as well as the right to food and availability of just markets. It is written more from a rural perspective, where most of the intractable poverty exists, and can be seen as a new blueprint for rural development policies. Unlike food security, which is a set of goals for food and nutrition policies, the Food Sovereignty framework is formulated as an alternative policy proposition to liberalized industrial agriculture and it amalgamates elements from different policy areas into one framework.

It covers issues which are already recognized in international law – e.g. the Right to Food – but also includes other aspects using rights-based language, which are so far not part of international law, such as 'the right to Food Sovereignty' or the 'right to produce'. The rights-based language is used to support the political demands by showing that these objectives have to be implemented to fulfil rights that are considered as basic by the affected communities. The framework covers the rights of individuals and the rights of all people at the same time. Even though both approaches are possible, more precision is needed in the use of the rights-based language. The political expansion of the rights-based language contains the risks for those rights, which are already legally binding, being seen more as political demands.

4

Potential for Food Sovereignty policies to eradicate poverty and hunger and to provide sustainable livelihoods

Any strategy recommendation for reducing rural poverty and supporting the development of sustainable livelihoods has to address, effectively, the causes of hunger and malnutrition and the barriers to rural development. The main causes and barriers fall into two groups: those more related to responsibilities of national policymaking and those more related to rules and policymaking at the international level. This distinction is not always easy to make, since in many countries national policymaking is heavily influenced by international framework conditions. Nevertheless, the differentiation is a useful methodological tool to enable a more precise discussion and identify the responsibilities of different actors. Without such an actor-oriented discussion, policy recommendations will not be specific enough to initiate the necessary changes. The causes of hunger at national levels can be summarized under five headings (see Table 2):

Marginalization

Central to the problem is that nearly half of the hungry people worldwide are smallholder farmers, pastoralists and fisherfolk who, to a very large extent, live and work on marginal land and in degraded coastal zones. The marginalization of these farmers is characterized by several elements. Many of them live in remote areas and suffer because of the long distance between them and basic infrastructure, such as local or national markets for selling their products. Often they also face fragile environmental conditions, as their land may be located in difficult environments for agriculture (arid, steep hills, etc.), often with poor soils and without access to irrigation. In addition, these farmers work under extremely difficult conditions, often lacking both capital and any support services from the state. Basic services for successful agricultural activities are seldom available. There is, therefore, a need for effective new rural policies to address the problems of marginalization.

The Food Sovereignty policy framework (subsequently called the Food Sovereignty framework) covers this problem in two ways. First, it stresses the problems of 'access to land' by smallholder farmers and pastoralists, and second it opts for a family farm / community-based rural development model that is based on agroecology, i.e. the sustainable use of available natural resources. This family farm/community-based model of agroecology is suggested as an alternative to the current trends of concentration of land and the control of other inputs (such as seeds and livestock breeds, pesticides, etc.) and outputs (marketable products).

The Food Sovereignty framework is effective in addressing the core problems of the marginalization of farms and, particularly, the management of the difficult fragile environmental situations of many smallholder farmers, pastoralists and fisherfolk through agroecology. Nevertheless, it depends on concrete policy objectives, which are not yet expressed in sufficient detail, before it will be possible to tell whether or not all aspects of marginalization will indeed be addressed. Moreover, while in the policy documents on Food Sovereignty the family farm/community agricultural model based on agroecology is presented as the new production methodology, the specific policy proposals focus more on the international dimension of the problems that smallholder farmers have. However, whether the problems that smallholder farmers on marginal land face are properly addressed or not depends on national policies.

Access to productive resources and land policy

The problem of marginalization is often caused or aggravated by other problems linked to the lack of, or insecure access to, productive resources. Access problems are particularly highlighted in the Food Sovereignty framework and cover issues such as access to land, water, agricultural biodiversity, traditional technology, etc. The current process of concentration of these assets, both inputs and markets, has had a huge detrimental impact on a family-farm-based model of agriculture. This is most evident in Europe and the US where the economic concentration process

Table 2 Major causes of hunger and barriers to rural poverty reduction relevant for the Food Sovereignty debate

Level	Major causes of hunger and barriers to rural poverty reduction
National	**1. Marginalization** • remoteness (from cities/markets and infrastructure) • fragile environmental conditions (soil quality, access to irrigation water, steep slopes, etc.) • access to services (agricultural extension services, credit, storage facilities, market access, etc.) **2. Access to productive resources and land policy** • security of land tenure vs. concentration of land • access to land for landless people, pastoralists and smallholder farmers • access to water and fishing grounds • access to agricultural biodiversity **3. Budget allocation** **4. Rural employment** • labour regulations • employment guarantee schemes **5. Other policy areas** • attracting foreign direct investment • privatization of essential services • extractive industries • HIV/Aids
International	**1. Prices / dumping** • export subsidies and similar forms of surplus disposal (e.g. food aid) • 'acquired' comparative advantages • other forms of market distortion **2. Markets** • concentration of companies • imperfect competition (monopolies, etc.) **3. Policy space** • conditionalities concerning budget allocations, land policies, extractive industry regulations, macro-economic guidance • possibilities of increasing regulation of corporations in the context of strong 'negotiation power of companies'

in the input and output side of agriculture has been most pronounced, but it is being replicated the world over.

Budget allocation

The quantity of development assistance and national budget allocation for the agricultural sector and to rural development has been decreasing for years, although this trend now seems to be reversing. This reflected a policy orientation that concentrated on overall poverty reduction measures, linked with the hope that the general poverty orientation of national policies would also reduce poverty in rural areas. Between 1986 and 1996, the budget allocation in most developing countries for rural development and for agriculture policies dropped by more than 50% in all developing countries, as well as in bi- and multi-lateral aid. Thus, the support for the already marginalized groups living in rural areas decreased considerably. The money that still goes into these areas predominantly supports commercial agriculture and competitive export sectors. The Food Sovereignty framework recognizes this neglect of smallholder farmers and other groups living in rural areas, such as pastoralists, fisherfolk and indigenous communities – who seldom get support from government policies – as a central issue. Nevertheless, the framework fails adequately to address this issue as an important element for future change or suggest how to include effective demands directed to national governments in Food Sovereignty strategies.

Rural employment

Some 22% of the hungry and malnourished are families and communities without access to productive resources, including landless and rural labourers. The Food Sovereignty framework highlights the problems of these groups, particularly the lack of access to land, water and other productive resources. The policy recommendations, however, do not address in detail the situation of rural labourers. Necessary policy recommendations would have to cover effective labour regulations as well as positive action to support rural employment, including employment guarantee schemes.

Other policy areas

Several other policy areas are particularly relevant to the causes of hunger, malnutrition and rural poverty, such as the active search for foreign direct investment (FDIs). In many developing countries FDIs lead to investment particularly in two sectors that are important for marginal groups living in rural areas. One is the investment in extractive industries that often have an extreme impact on changing land-use patterns, particularly where surface mining is concerned. Extractive industries also have huge environmental impacts on water streams, soil quality and pollution (in the case of spillages, etc.). The other sector is the privatization of essential services, such as water supply. Even if most of the Food Sovereignty literature does not address these problems directly, it does in principle insist on the right of peoples and nations to determine their own policies. One of the essential arguments of Food Sovereignty is that there is a need to rebuild capacity and policy spaces to control policies that affect the lives of rural populations. On the other hand there is not enough discussion about whether the national policy level is even able to deliver local ownership policies, as in many countries there are huge conflicts between local autonomy and national centralized power. This is the 'internal' risk of any local sovereignty strategy.

International economic influences

Which international influences most affect national policies and could be responsible for causing hunger, malnutrition or rural poverty? The following list, while not comprehensive, attempts to summarize the most important ones:

Prices and dumping

A core problem for smallholder farmers in many countries is that imported competing agricultural products are often sold worldwide at prices below the cost of production. There are several ways to subsidize exports. Most criticized are direct export subsidies,[22] but other hidden export subsidies are equally important, such as some food aid and the practices of some marketing boards.[23] The indirect effects of subsidizing agricultural producers also contribute to the trend of depressed prices: subsidies paid in industrialized countries foster structural overproduction there, which has to be either destroyed or exported. So even subsidies not directly linked to exports might depress world market prices. It has been calculated that in 2000 some US$245 billion was spent by industrialized countries to subsidize their agriculture (Oxfam International, 2002 p.112).[24] Long-term subsidies for large farms in industrialized countries lead, in the long run, to 'acquired comparative advantages', as the OECD describes these gains in competitiveness.

The problem of cheap imports is often subsumed under the headline of 'dumping'. Via Campesina defines dumping as the sale of products at less than their cost of production in the countries of origin and destination. Ending dumping – which creates some of the most damaging international impacts on smallholder farmers all over the world – is, therefore, a key concern for Food Sovereignty policies. The demands presented in the Food Sovereignty debate with regard to dumping go further than the mere elimination of export or other subsidies paid to agriculture in the North. At the national level it calls for measures to protect local producers against unfair competition, and at the international level it calls for unjust subsidies to be removed and policies at national level that enable the supply management of food.

Unfair competition

It is often assumed that markets function efficiently, while in reality they are often poorly regulated and do not serve weaker participants. The problems of smallholder farmers often start with lack of access to inputs, partly because of their remoteness, but mainly because of market concentration in the input sector, with a few companies focusing on the needs of intensive agriculture and ignoring the needs of smallholder farmers in many rural areas. Governments also tend not to support agricultural research and extension services relevant to the smallholder sector, further reducing access to inputs such as appropriate seeds and livestock breeds, weather forecasts, etc. Smallholder's problems are further aggravated by the physical lack of access to markets for their produce. The absence of infrastructure for transport or storage often forces smallholders to sell their produce at harvest, when prices are lowest. This means that middlemen who buy and store the produce get most of the eventual revenue. State trading enterprises or other forms of state support to overcome these problems of access to market for smallholder farmers are under pressure from international trade rules and policies driven by many richer countries to reduce their activities.[25] Additionally, there is such strong concentration among the agricultural trading companies, grain marketing organizations, and the food industry that it leads inevitably to imperfect competition.

The lost role of the nation state

One of the main problems highlighted by promoters of Food Sovereignty is the loss of governments' authority to regulate important national policy areas such as trade, biodiversity and even land policy. The policy space for a nation's own decisions is increasingly reduced, since international norms are prescribing what is possible at the national level. This is particularly visible in WTO agreements. In the past, the GATT system was comparatively limited in the areas of agricultural policy that it influenced. Since the establishment of the WTO, however, and the package deal that was agreed at the end of the Uruguay Round, a set of agreements with many subsidiary agreements was adopted. These agreements regulate many areas – from food quality, to classification of additives, labelling, rules of origin, patents, etc. – which earlier had been regulated by national policies.

In addition to international agreements such as trade agreements, many developing countries are also heavily influenced by policy conditionality and advice given by the World Bank and the IMF through structural adjustment programmes or poverty reduction strategies. It is important to note that while not all World Bank and IMF recommendations are mandatory, some constitute strict conditions often linked to debt re-scheduling and macroeconomic guidance, such as the opening of markets for agricultural products, etc. These conditions influence decisions on budget allocations, on how to run certain policy areas, such as land policies, and on how to regulate certain types of industrial activity, such as extractive industry regulations. Moreover, governments' limited opportunities to regulate their own national policies are dictated by the strong negotiating power of foreign companies. Countries seeking to attract foreign direct investment have only a small margin of discretion in which to set standards for investment on local content provisions or employment regulation. The particular strength of the Food Sovereignty framework is that the problem of decreasing state regulatory power is addressed. Part of the essence of the Food Sovereignty framework is to regain policy space for national policymaking. On the other hand, whether the state can regain that power in times of globalization still needs to be addressed.

The Food Sovereignty framework includes recommendations concerning national policy setting with respect to all of the problem areas identified. Nevertheless, when it comes to the policy proposals and strategies, the framework has a slight bias towards policy changes at the international level. The main focus is to widen policy spaces for the nation state in international regimes such as the trade regime. National responsibilities are not addressed in as detailed a way as international trade policy changes. Even though policy areas particularly influenced by the nation state, such as the overall agricultural policy orientation and budget recommendations, are recognized, they are not fully addressed, particularly when it comes to concrete policy proposals. The framework first and foremost aims to create policy space for the nation state in international forums, assuming that they would be adopted by national governments. Whether, and under what conditions, national governments would make use of these policy spaces for the benefit of hungry and malnourished peoples has not yet been thoroughly discussed. While conditions are indeed often heavily influenced by international policies, nevertheless more and better-defined changes should be demanded at the national level as well. In many countries national polices still play an important role and should therefore not be downplayed.

5

Analysis of constraints to the adoption and implementation of Food Sovereignty policies

Advocates of Food Sovereignty support it particularly because they see the need to reformulate core elements of the current model of rural development. It is never easy to advocate for substantial changes in a policy area, since proof is needed that the current model is not working properly or is either producing a negative outcome or too many unintended side effects.

The Food Sovereignty framework recognizes that those living in farming, fishing and herding communities need special support to overcome the problems of hunger, malnutrition and rural poverty in an environmentally sustainable way. It asserts that the current model is unable substantially to reduce the number of people who are hungry or malnourished. However, while the current system still seems to be productive in terms of global output, there are problems with the distribution of benefits to poor and hungry people and its unsustainable production methods lead to the marginalization of smallholder farmers and to long-term environmental threats. An urgent re-evaluation of agricultural and rural policies is, therefore, required to reverse these negative trends. It should no longer be acceptable to assert that more growth in agricultural output (and more overall economic growth) will automatically deliver substantial benefits to all people living in rural areas.

It is possible to identify six constraints and counter arguments that can be used to challenge the framework:

1. The first challenge is from the current dominant development paradigms which are built on a combination of elements that can be grouped under three headings:

    (a) political preconditions such as democracy, good governance, and no corruption;

    (b) the macro-economic policy model based on open markets and trade-based food security;[26] and

    (c) the current development or social policy agenda which is driving the achievement of the Millennium Development Goals (MDGs), which also contain elements of (a) and (b).

The Food Sovereignty framework is a counter proposal to the neo-liberal macro-economic policy framework. It is not directed against trade *per se*, but is based on the reality that current international trade practices and trade rules are not working in favour of smallholder farmers. While the opening up of markets in developed countries is a key demand of many development NGOs, the Food Sovereignty framework is asking for the right of nations and peoples to restrict trade, if this is needed to protect smallholder farmers and other rural marginalized communities against dumping and unfair competition. The focus of Food Sovereignty is to guarantee trading conditions that are not threatening to smallholder farmers. Many Food Sovereignty advocates, for example Via Campesina, reject the policy proposals to reform the WTO by limiting trade under certain conditions, such as by using a 'development box' (i.e. giving developing countries certain exemptions), although this is supported by some developing countries. Via Campesina fears that Food Sovereignty could then be implemented under WTO rules, which would still require acceptance of the basic principles of the WTO, such as liberalization, non-discrimination and the 'most favoured nation' clause. On the other hand, Food Sovereignty is not an anti-trade policy, but implies rather a demand for a trade system based on fundamentally different principles, such as those that promote local trade and a careful and controlled opening of markets.

2. The second challenge comes from those who focus more on a global food security perspective, using arguments that are more production oriented. For many years the focus of agricultural policies was on increasing global production through the latest technology, using high-yielding varieties and optimal application of inputs and irrigation. This has increased global food production steadily during the last half century and has prevented steep rises in the number of hungry and malnourished people, while the world population has been increasing. Many questions remain, however. Will smallholder farmers, pastoralists and fisherfolk be able to increase global production enough, particularly if support for marginal farmers is combined with agroecology? Will a new policy based on the interests of smallholder farmers, pastoralists and fisherfolk adequately take into account the future need to increase the production of food for the growing world population? Is there a risk that Food Sovereignty policies will favour producers who are less 'efficient' in conventional economic terms?

In fact, it seems that the focus of Food Sovereignty on rural communities and smallholder family farms is, from time to time, supported by experts analysing the causes of hunger and malnutrition. The Millennium Project's Hunger Task Force was, for example, arguing: '*For higher risk environments, a different paradigm focused more on the interplay between locally developed agricultural technologies and improved natural resource management is developing*' (UNDP, 2003b, p.9). The Task Force authors also highlighted how important it will be to focus future strategies on *locally adapted* technologies, though this was not carried through to recommendations in their final report (UNDP, 2005).

It has been shown that the yields of smallholdings, even in higher risk environments, can be increased three- or fourfold using locally adapted techniques. Therefore, in any future strategy to increase world food output it will be more appropriate to focus research on smallholder farmers, including those in marginal environments. Moreover, an increasing number of studies support the need to develop more diverse agricultural farming practices for all types of production systems based on agroecology, systems in which food production, biological support systems such as pollination and pest control, and ecosystem services such as clean water, soil conservation and watershed protection are recognized as important outputs of farming landscapes (Altieri, 1995).

3. Another challenge to the Food Sovereignty framework is linked particularly to the use of the term 'sovereignty'. The challenge is twofold:

   (1) Is the use of the term still possible in times of globalization? Is it not an outmoded, quasi-romantic point of view that does not recognize the need to open up economies and the need for the international exchange of ideas, goods, services, tourism, etc?

   (2) Is it still useful to refer to the nation state as an agent for policy development, or is the nation state already becoming too weak? The modern

dilemma of the nation state has been eloquently reduced one sentence statement in the *UNDP Human Development Report 2000*: '*The nation state is too big for the small things and too small for the big things.*' How useful can Food Sovereignty policies be in times when those policies' governance mechanism, the nation state, is becoming weaker and weaker?

The first answer to these profound challenges is that Food Sovereignty does not primarily refer to nation-state sovereignty. A new and modern definition of sovereignty is found in the different interpretations of Food Sovereignty. Sovereignty is used to demand the right to control policies, the distribution of resources, and national and international decision-making for those who are directly affected by these policies. The term has therefore a much connotation of local democracy, participatory development, and subsidiarity than of national policy formulation and government bureaucracies. Nevertheless, one can also find texts on Food Sovereignty that focus more on the 'rights of peoples and nations' than local communities.

One of the open questions in the debate is what is really meant by the term Food Sovereignty? The different texts dealing with Food Sovereignty do not use a consistent definition (see appendix) but all require greater democracy in determining localized food and agricultural systems. Food Sovereignty highlights the negative interference from international policies on the lives of local communities and smallholder farmers, pastoralists and fisherfolk and the need to re-assert local autonomy in order to solve the problems of poverty and hunger. But it has also been used to make clear that the role of the nation state is still important and that it is necessary to carefully reconsider what should be regulated locally, nationally and internationally. Food Sovereignty is a call to remind us that the process of globalization itself is a political process that can be changed. It is also a call to encourage and foster a discussion on different and alternative options for future policy development in the agricultural sector that are not entirely dominated by the globalization project. It is demanding a development model that gives the control of resources back to local communities. Nevertheless, a potential conflict remains between the advantages of local control and sovereignty and the advantages of open-mindedness to new internationally controlled policies.

4. The Food Sovereignty framework is challenged by the question about the need for more global governance. How much 'global governance' is needed in the future is an ongoing debate in international relations and among NGOs/CSOs and social movements? Would it not be wiser to invest more energy in developing the right international instruments instead of focusing on sovereignty and improved democracy at national or even local levels? One of the advantages of the Food Sovereignty framework is that it addresses both new international regulations and the need to decentralize decision-making to local or national levels. The central message of Food Sovereignty is that the revitalization of rural development and rural policies needs to be secured in international policies.

5. Is there any space for new conventions or new legal instruments to ensure Food Sovereignty? In the different texts about Food Sovereignty several proposals are made for new international legal instruments (see p.15) such as a convention on Food Sovereignty; an international treaty on the rights of smallholder farmers, pastoralists and fisherfolk (see appendix for summary); a new World Commission on Sustainable Agriculture and Food Sovereignty; a reformed and a strengthened United Nations; and a new dispute settlement mechanism. The variety of instruments and the scope of the proposed changes are considerable.

Would it be more appropriate to design limited policy proposals set in a realistic timeframe, instead of proposing radical changes in the current system of the United Nations? This is a key question for all the strategic recommendations that are made about Food Sovereignty. It can be argued that the instruments that have been proposed so far are not a coherent package, but rather a list of incomplete ideas, and thus are not entirely useful. What all supporters of Food Sovereignty stress are that drastic changes are needed in many policy areas to implement this new policy framework and reduce hunger and poverty. However, Food Sovereignty is not yet sufficiently defined and established as a conceptual framework to be able to decide precisely which legal instruments and infrastructure will be required to support it at national or international levels.

6. The Food Sovereignty framework is confused in its use of the term human rights. The problem is that two different ways of applying the concepts of 'rights' are being mixed up. First of all, it is stated that the right to food is a fundamental human right for each individual and community. This human right needs to be established separately from the more conceptual form of the word 'right' in a political context: the right to produce food or the right to Food Sovereignty is so far not internationally recognized. It would be helpful to separate the political use of the rights terminology from the legal one, since the right to food, an established international instrument, can already be claimed in courts. The right to food covers particular rules and regulations for states vis-à-vis people living in their territory, but also includes extraterritorial obligations.

Food Sovereignty poses political challenges, which require that states should regain the necessary policy space to conduct their fight against hunger and to be able to implement fully their obligations to their citizens to ensure both their Right to Adequate Food as well as their other human rights. Moreover, states should provide an environment that facilitates the implementation of all human rights obligations. However, the availability of the necessary policy space does not automatically lead to national policies that promote or even consider the interests of smallholder farmers, pastoralists and fisherfolk or remote rural areas, because national governments are often not respectful of the needs of the poorer segments of their society. The right to food is, therefore, an extremely important additional element, since it is a way to make accountable national governments to people facing hunger and malnutrition.

To summarize, the Food Sovereignty framework paves the way for special attention to be given to the international governance of food and agriculture and to the international causes of hunger and malnutrition. It also encourages a discussion about the policy space that needs to exist to encourage (but not necessarily guarantee) the creation of national policies that aim to reduce rural poverty and eliminate hunger and malnutrition. The right to adequate food, however, is a legal reference instrument and provides legal standards for all measures and policies undertaken by each state to secure access to adequate food for everyone. It requires that the policy space available is used properly and that states implement their obligations to both the right to adequate food and other human rights.

The key to reducing hunger, malnutrition and rural poverty is a renewed focus on rural development and rural areas. Even in the next four decades the majority of the poor will live in rural areas. The Food Sovereignty framework constitutes an important contribution to the current discussion by directly addressing the needs and demands of those who face hunger and malnutrition, and so merits further elaboration.

6

Extent of recognition of Food Sovereignty by governments, intergovernmental organizations, civil society organizations and social movements

Despite the fact that the Food Sovereignty framework is still evolving, it is increasingly being recognized. Already at the parallel NGO forum at the World Food Summit in 1996, the concept of Food Sovereignty was widely supported among NGOs/CSOs and social movements. For these organizations, Food Sovereignty has become the central policy framework within which they operate. Moreover, the farmers' organizations linked to Via Campesina have fully adopted Food Sovereignty as the basis for their struggle. However, some other farmer organizations and some NGOs do not yet support the concept. For many it is still unknown, for others some of the challenges mentioned in previous chapters have not been answered adequately.

Among governments the concept received some early support in 1988 when a group of developing countries used it in the negotiations on agriculture during the Uruguay Round. In fact, representatives from developing countries suggested that Food Sovereignty would be preferable to food security.[27] The three elements of this interpretation of Food Sovereignty mentioned by the sponsoring governments were (i) national self-determination of what was produced and how it was produced; (ii) a guarantee of sufficient supply at adequate prices and availability, and (iii) incentives to rural and national development on the basis of increasing production, consumption, and the income of producers. Since then, the term has sometimes been used in trade negotiations, particularly in meetings in which the introduction of a 'development box' has been discussed. Nevertheless, one cannot find any recent references to countries using the term Food Sovereignty.

Within the European Parliament, advocates such as the Committee on Women's Rights and Equal Opportunities have urged the European Commission to introduce the use of the term 'Food Sovereignty' alongside that of food security. The term is being used to a limited extent by official decision-makers in the EU and FAO, but some seem to use it in a different way than civil society does. There is a real risk that the framework will be watered down and lose its initial meaning, or become interchangeable with Food Security. During the WTO Ministerial Conference in Cancun in September, 2003 the Belgian Minister of Foreign Affairs stated that the Belgian government welcomed the recent EU reform of the Common Agricultural Policy, and argued that it would make a powerful contribution to the Food Sovereignty of the countries of the South, while promoting their agricultural production and export. To this end, he continued, *'rules need to be adopted to provide developing countries with the means for better integration [into] international trade'*. Therefore, the full achievement of the Doha Development Agenda is crucial, he concluded. This shows that so far no one definition of the term exists, and that it is already being used in ways that are quite contrary to the spirit of the original meaning. In particular the appealing tone of the word 'sovereignty' will make it attractive for many to (mis)use the term, without a specific context. An important task for NGOs and CSOs, therefore, is to publicise and advocate for the definition that they have agreed and to gain support for it not only inside civil society, but also among governments.

It is easy to foresee problems in achieving more political support, particularly since the framework is broad and covers a variety of issues and proposals. New thinking on agricultural and rural development policies is required, but paradigm shifts need time. Many people might agree with the principles of Food Sovereignty, but disagree with some of the analyses or policy proposals. Moreover, the framework is still in development. Although we can see a convergence in the analyses of important problems, concrete policy proposals still have to be developed and defined further. On a global level, we are still in a phase of influencing agendas in international fora, where the framework is receiving increased recognition. To encourage this discussion, a parallel event to the 2003 meeting of the FAO Committee on World Food Security was organized between civil society organizations, FAO and some government representatives.

Nevertheless, we are still far away from finding broad political support among governments because of the radical changes that have taken place, particularly when it comes to trade policy issues. While few will disagree with Food Sovereignty's principle of the human right to food, some countries will remain opposed to the overall framework. When it comes to reducing resistance to Food Sovereignty, however, its comprehensive nature could be an advantage. The policy changes needed to reduce the number of hungry and malnourished as well as to tackle rural poverty in the foreseeable future are enormous. A broad-based discussion is more likely to initiate far-reaching changes than a discussion about making small changes to existing instruments.

7
Current relevance of Food Sovereignty

The current problems of hunger and malnutrition, as well as rural poverty, are an unavoidable challenge for international policy. They have received some attention internationally, for example the adoption of the first Millennium Development Goal, which built on the Rome Declaration adopted at the 1996 World Food Summit to reduce by half the number of hungry people by 2015, and changes in some bi- and multi-lateral aid policies of OECD countries, but so far the results have been negative. FAO's data for 1999–2001 shows that there are actually 18 million more severely undernourished people since 1995–7 (FAO 2003c), and that increased still further during the subsequent three years. In 2004 there were 852 million severely undernourished people in the world.

This negative trend shows that policy change is needed. FAO analysis still maintains that the failure to reduce the number of hungry and malnourished people is a result of lack of political will. Nevertheless, it is not only a question of political will, but also a question of identifying new policies or reforming or eliminating perverse policies.

The central questions of the current debate need to be:

- How do we to mobilize more political will to address the root causes of hunger and poverty?

- How do we set up policy conditions that would lead to a substantial reduction in the number of hungry and malnourished people in the foreseeable future?

- What policy changes are needed and feasible?

The current dominant policies for eliminating hunger and malnutrition are evidently not working and need to be changed. Food Sovereignty is not a luxury or a utopian dream, but a necessity. A change of attitude and approach, at all levels of policymaking, that prioritizes the needs and security of smallholder farmers, pastoralists and fisherfolk the world over should be a political and social priority. Additional analysis and a search for new, more innovative answers are needed. The current main policy options are:

1. The seven commitments agreed in the Plan of Action (PoA) from the World Food Summit (and incorporated into the first MDG). This contains a long list of good ideas but has not been developed into a concrete plan of action, nor does it tackle the contradictions between different elements of the action plan.

2. A faster and more wide-ranging liberalization of agricultural markets in order to end the devastating impact of the current market distortions – the WTO's Doha Development Agenda.

Both of these mainstream policy options address key issues and make important proposals for changes. But even the implementation of the World Food Summit

Plan of Action would not change policy enough to end hunger and malnutrition. Even worse, some of these proposals might result in more vulnerable people or groups: further liberalizing the market in agricultural products, for example.

Two important components are neglected in the current mainstream approaches:

1. National and international policy changes need to be made in the right order. The mainstream policy advice is for increased investment in the agricultural sector and in rural areas at both national and international level. Developing countries are to be encouraged to open up their markets for agricultural products. It is not sufficiently acknowledged, however, that this liberalization requires a level playing field of competitive markets with producers capable of taking advantage of these. Considering that most poor and hungry people are rural smallholder farmers, pastoralists and fisherfolk who have no external support and require increased capacity to access markets, opening up their local markets to international competition would quickly drive them out of production altogether. Before they are exposed to global competition, they first need increased recognition of their contribution to food security and effective support that would enable them to be able to compete in an open market. The need for government to support these smallholder (and often marginalized) farmers and landless families is too often forgotten.

   In terms of the order in which policies are implemented, opening up markets before smallholder farmers, pastoralists and fisherfolk have the capacity to exploit them will not benefit these producers. This damage would be even more severe were the markets of developing countries to be opened before the market-distorting effects of subsidies on the agricultural production and exports of industrialized countries are reformed. A substantial reduction of subsidies is still a long way away, but many developing countries have already opened their markets, so it is not surprising that farmer's movements around the world are calling for the implementation of Food Sovereignty policies.

2. Important vulnerable groups are not covered by the policy advice given.
   The analysis of people facing hunger and malnutrition as well as extreme poverty has shown that the majority are living in rural areas and are landless families or smallholder farmers, pastoralists or fisherfolk. Most of these families will need long-term support before they could even contemplate accessing international markets: they would have to be supported first to market their products locally and in regional markets. The current economic policy option to address this is specialization and support for structural changes to move farmers away from agricultural production that is not 'competitive'. Although in macro-economic terms this might have some validity for some people in the long term, it does not address how hundreds of millions of smallholder farmers, pastoralists and fisherfolk and landless families will find alternative jobs. It is the essence of the problem of hunger and poverty that economic options other than agriculture are not available in the short term. Jobs for the increasing rural population have to be created through agriculture and the sustainable use of natural resources, and through the local and regional processing of agricultural products. The failure to pay attention to this reality explains, in part, the growing number of hungry and malnourished people in the world.

The purpose of this paper has shown how Food Sovereignty framework developed and has explained the basic assumptions and underlying analyses. It has described how the framework relates to the current problems in rural and agricultural policies and has discussed what policy constraints might prevent the adoption of the framework.

It has shown that the common thread of all the different interpretations of Food Sovereignty is that their analyses start from the perspective of those facing hunger and rural poverty. The debate on the different instruments and their potential has been documented in this paper, but has only recently started among the different civil society actors. It is a dynamic debate that needs to be supported and enriched by more civil society and scientific contributions, because finding credible and effective answers to the overall problem will not be an easy task. It is likely that the Food Sovereignty framework could best be developed by implementing several of the ideas in parallel. Some initiatives have already begun, for example some co-ordination of views is being achieved in the IPC for Food Sovereignty. For the time being the most important outcome could be to enrich the debate and discuss the relevance of different potential policy changes. Each NGO, civil society organization or social movement should then decide which strategic elements it can support.

This paper shows that there is no one fully fledged 'Food Sovereignty model' in the sense of a set of policies already available for the national and global governance of rural and agricultural policies. Even though many key elements of such a new proposal have already been identified and formulated, the overall framework and strategy needs further improvement and clarification, as this paper has shown. The use of terminology and definitions, particularly the rights-based language, needs to be more precise. Several issues have so far not been addressed properly by this policy framework, such as the situation of the urban poor and their access to food. These are areas in which further debate is needed. The framework has not yet been finalized: it is still in development.

Food Sovereignty is the new policy framework being developed by social movements all over the world to improve the governance of food and agriculture and to fight the core problems of hunger and poverty in new and innovative ways. It deserves serious consideration and more discussion on how to develop it further.

Endnotes

1   Subsequently the terms 'farmer' or 'smallholder farmers, pastoralists and fisherfolk' will be used in this paper for all those women and men who produce and harvest crops as well as livestock and aquatic organisms. This should be understood to include smallholder peasant/family crop and livestock farmers, herders/ pastoralists, artisanal fisherfolk, landless farmers/ rural workers, gardeners, indigenous peoples, and hunters and gatherers, among other small-scale users of natural resources for food production.

2   The persistence of the problem is easily observed; at the World Food Conference in 1974 government representatives declared that in ten years 'no child will have to go to bed hungry'.

3   Officially the FAO estimated before the WFS:*fyl* that the number of hungry people had fallen by six million a year between 1996 and 2002. Even at the summit it was doubtful whether the figures were reliable, because the numbers were based on a reduction of hungry people in China, while at the same time the number of hungry people had increased in many other countries. In between, the FAO had to adjust the figures again to more than 840 million. No progress has been made in reducing the total number since the WFS in 1996.

4   FAO estimates the underfunding to be in the order of US$24 billion (FAO, 2002a).

5   This first report was published in New York in April 2003 (see: http://millen niumindicators.un.org/unsd/mi/mi_goals.asp). See also the excellent overview by the International Fund for Agricultural Development, *Rural Poverty Report 2001. The Challenge of Ending Rural Poverty* (IFAD, 2001).

6   This issue has been documented by the former director of the World Watch Institute, Lester Brown. The most recent figures can be found in World Watch Institute (2003). 'Producing meat requires large amounts of grain – most of the corn and soybean harvested in the world are used to fatten livestock. Producing 1 calorie of meat (beef, pork, or chicken) requires 11–17 calories of feed. So a meat-eater's diet requires two to four times more land than a vegetarian's diet' (p.30).

7   The Millennium Project (UNDP, 2003a, p.16–22) describes in detail how marginal many farming areas are today. Marginal in the sense of rural remoteness and distance to roads, infrastructure and markets and marginal in terms of policy in national and international agendas.

8   The average budget for rural development in developing countries was reduced by 50% between the mid-1980s and mid-1990s. The same happened to bi- and multilateral aid. The World Bank, for example, dropped its lending to these sectors from nearly US$6 billion in 1986 to US$2.7 billion in 1996. Many reasons are given for this decline, including among others: the inherent

complexity, risk, and relatively high transaction costs in agriculture and rural development projects (particularly with poor producers); an aversion among Bank staff and clients to lending in those sectors; and the low effectiveness of institutions working with these sectors in many countries (see FAO, 2001).

9   The problem of dumping subsidized exports and the impact of trade distortions linked to subsidies are well documented by UN, the OECD and also by NGO documents (see Oxfam, 2002).

10   Recent price trends on the world market are quite low. See the good overview in BMVEL (2004). Additionally all price trends are published regularly by the FAO.

11   Colin Hines (2003) has described how globalization is transforming the diversity of food systems into an integrated and more linear world system.

12   The 'Global Convention on Food Security' later became the 'International Convention on Food Sovereignty and Nutritional Well-Being' (Havana, 2001), or the International Convention on Food Sovereignty and Trade (Cancun, 2003).

13   The IPC for Food Sovereignty is a network consisting of a more than 2000 NGOs, CSOs and social movements, emanating from an international consultation and interaction process that began in 2000, and which built on the networks started at the WFS in 1996.

14   The definition was elaborated during the WFS:*fyl* parallel NGO/CSO forum (Forum for Food Sovereignty) and can be found on the fact sheet on Food Sovereignty on the homepage of the IPC at www.foodsovereignty.org.

15   The draft was prepared by both the People's Food Sovereignty Network Asia Pacific, a new regional coalition of peasant-farmer organizations and support NGOs, working on a platform of Food Sovereignty, and the Pesticide Action Network Asia and the Pacific. The text is available on PAN-AP's website: www.panap.net

16   The Right to Food is recognized in Art. 25 of the Universal Declaration of Human Rights (UDHR) and in Art. 11 of the International Covenant on Economic, Social and Cultural Rights (ICESCR). In both texts it is part of the right to an adequate standard of living. Art. 11 also recognizes the right to be free from hunger.

17   The notion of 'individual entitlement' does not exclude the possibility that in many circumstances individual rights are only enjoyed in communities, such as in indigenous communities. It therefore does not exclude common land title of communities, etc. It is important that the right can be claimed through the courts and that responsible institutions can be held accountable.

18   General Comment No.12 is an interpretative note for the Right to Food adopted in May, 1999 by the UN Committee on Economic, Social and Cultural Rights. These types of Comments are drafted by all human rights treaty bodies that monitor state compliance with the central UN human rights treaties. General Comment No.12 is referenced as UN Doc. E/C.12/1999/5. Also relevant to the Right to Food is General Comment No.15 of the same Committee on the 'Right to Water', UN Doc. E/C.12/2002/11, adopted in 2002, which contains the Right to drinking water as part of the Right to Food.

19   The newly created network of CSOs, social movements and NGOs for economic, social and cultural rights (ESCR-Net) has set up a database on case-

related information. Currently more than 80 court cases involving ESC Rights are documented there. It can be accessed on the webpage of the network: www.escr-net.org. Some of the cases are related to the Right to Food.

20 The definition is included in paragraph 1 of the World Food Summit Plan of Action (FAO, 1996). FIVIMS is a tool developed in response to the World Food Summit results. A technical consultation on Food Insecurity and Vulnerability Information and Mapping Systems (FIVIMS) was held at the FAO in March 1997. It recommended developing guidelines for the establishment of FIVIMS at the national level. The guidelines were published in 2000 (IAGW-FIVIMS, 2000).

21 The Plan of Action, for example, recommends support to smallholder farmers in many of its chapters. However, the potential conflicts with the free trade paradigm that is also recommended are not discussed, neither in the document, nor in the Committee on World Food Security, which is the FAO body in charge of monitoring the implementation of the WFS.

22 The problem with the size of export subsidies using data from 2001 are described in detail in the study *Rigged Rules and Double Standards: Trade globalization, and the fight against poverty* (Oxfam, 2002, p.112ff).

23 The 'misuse' of food aid was discussed at an international conference in Berlin called 'Politics against hunger'. For details see: www.foodaid-berlin2003.de/

24 The figure deserves discussion: it is based on the OECD PSE (producer support estimate) which includes direct subsidies as well as negative subsidization (the costs to consumers, who have to pay higher prices). Although these estimates may be inflated, it shows that many subsidies go directly to trading and storage companies. The *actual* amount of subsidies paid directly to farmers in the EU and the US will be lower than these figures suggest.

25 See monthly updates on the negotiations in *Bridges*, a magazine published by the International Centre for Trade and Sustainable Development (www.ictsd.org).

26 The model is most often called 'neo-liberal'. While there is now consistent use of the term neo-liberal, here the basic components have been identified separately in order to be more precise.

27 The proposal was submitted by Egypt, Jamaica, Mexico and Peru, supported by Morocco and Nigeria. See document MTG.GNG/NG5/W/74 of the GATT-Uruguay-Round documents.

28 Linked to the principle of protecting natural resources in the Food Sovereignty discourse, the discussion of a model of production should be based on agricultural biodiversity and not on an industrial model: 'Food Sovereignty and security, livelihoods, landscapes and environmental integrity are underpinned by agricultural biodiversity and its component genetic resources for food and agriculture. These have been developed by indigenous peoples and women and men farmers, forest dwellers, livestock keepers and fisherfolk over the past 12,000 years through the free exchange of genetic resources across the world. Since the advent of industrial agriculture and the increasing globalization of markets, tastes and cultures, much of this wealth of agricultural biodiversity is being lost both on-farm and in genebanks and increasingly the integrity of these resources is being compromised by

genetically modified organisms.' (Quote from the background paper to the WFS:*fyl* CSO Forum for Food Sovereignty 'Sustaining Agricultural Biodiversity'.)

29 The Cartagena Protocol on Biosafety became law and entered into force on September 11, 2003.

30 The draft was prepared by the People´s Food Sovereignty Network Asia Pacific, a new regional coalition of peasant–farmer organizations and support NGOs who working on a platform of Food Sovereignty, as well as the Pestcide Action Network Asia and the Pacific. The text is available on the web-site of PAN-AP: www.panap.net.

Appendix

Food Sovereignty: Historical overview of the development of the concept

The concept of Food Sovereignty, that had been under discussion for a few years, was released as a result of the International Conference of Via Campesina in Tlaxcala, Mexico, in April 1996. Delegates decided that they wanted proper representation at the International Technical Conference on Plant Genetic Resources in Leipzig (Germany) in June 1996, as well as the Word Food Summit in Rome in November of the same year and in the parallel CSO forums. The objective was to encourage NGOs and CSOs to discuss alternatives to the neo-liberal proposals for achieving food security.

> *'We, the Via Campesina, a growing movement of farm workers, peasant, farm and indigenous peoples' organizations from all the regions of the world, know that food security cannot be achieved without taking full account of those who produce food. Any discussion that ignores our contribution will fail to eradicate poverty and hunger. Food is a basic human right. This right can only be realized in a system where* Food Sovereignty *is guaranteed.' (Via Campesina, 1996b).*

This definition of Food Sovereignty focuses on the right of smallholder farmers to produce food, which is undermined in many countries by national and international agricultural trade policy regulations. As discussed in this paper, for most developing countries these rules have been dictated either by structural adjustment programmes or by the WTO. In the words of Via Campesina, Food Sovereignty is *'the right of each nation to maintain and develop their own capacity to produce foods that are crucial to national and community food security, respecting cultural diversity and diversity of production methods.'*

During the 1996 World Food Summit, Via Campesina presented a set of requirements that offered an alternative to the world trade policies and would realize the human right to food. In the statement, 'Food Sovereignty: A Future without Hunger' (1996b), it was declared that *'Food Sovereignty is a precondition to genuine food security'*, and the right to food can therefore be seen as the tool to achieve it. Since this document has served as a basis for other declarations to come, Via Campesina's seven principles to achieve Food Sovereignty are worth highlighting:

1. ***Food – A Basic Human Right***
   Food is a basic human right. Everyone must have access to safe, nutritious and culturally appropriate food in sufficient quantity and quality to sustain a healthy life with full human dignity. Each nation should declare that access to food is a constitutional right and guarantee the development of the primary sector to ensure the concrete realization of this fundamental right.

2. ***Agrarian Reform***
   A genuine agrarian reform is necessary which gives landless and farming people – especially women – ownership and control of the land they work and returns territories

to indigenous peoples. The right to land must be free of discrimination on the basis of gender religion, race, social class or ideology; the land belongs to those who work it. Smallholder farmer families, especially women, must have access to productive land, credit, technology, markets and extension services. Governments must establish and support decentralized rural credit systems that prioritize the production of food for domestic consumption to ensure Food Sovereignty. Production capacity rather than land should be used as security to guarantee credit. To encourage young people to remain in rural communities as productive citizens, the work of producing food and caring for the land has to be sufficiently valued both economically and socially. Governments must make long-term investments of public resources in the development of socially and ecologically appropriate rural infrastructure.

3. Protecting Natural Resources
Food Sovereignty entails the sustainable care and use of natural resources especially land, water, and seeds and livestock breeds. The people who work the land must have the right to practice sustainable management of natural resources and to preserve biological diversity. This can only be done from a sound economic basis with security of tenure, healthy soils and reduced use of agro-chemicals. Long-term sustainability demands a shift away from dependence on chemical inputs, on cash-crop monocultures and intensive, industrialized production models. Balanced and diversified natural systems are required. Genetic resources are the result of millennia of evolution and belong to all of humanity. They represent the careful work and knowledge of many generations of rural and indigenous peoples. The patenting and commercialization of genetic resources by private companies must be prohibited. The WTO's Intellectual Property Rights Agreement is therefore unacceptable. Farming communities have the right to freely use and protect the diverse genetic resources, including seeds and livestock breeds, which have been developed by them throughout history.[28]

4. Reorganizing Food Trade
Food is first and foremost a source of nutrition and only secondarily an item of trade. National agricultural policies must prioritize production for domestic consumption and food self-sufficiency. Food imports must not displace local production nor depress prices. This means that export dumping or subsidized exports must cease. Smallholder farmers have the right to produce essential food staples for their countries and to control the marketing of their products. Food prices in domestic and international markets must be regulated and reflect the true costs of producing that food. This would ensure that smallholder farmer families have adequate incomes. It is unacceptable that the trade in food commodities continues to be based on the economic exploitation of the most vulnerable – the lowest earning producers – and the further degradation of the environment. It is equally unacceptable that trade and production decisions are increasingly dictated by the need for foreign currency to meet high debt loads. These debts place a disproportionate burden on rural people and should therefore be forgiven.

5. Ending the Globalization of Hunger
Food Sovereignty is undermined by multilateral institutions and by speculative capital. The growing control of multinational corporations over agricultural policies has been facilitated by the economic policies of multilateral organizations such as WTO, World Bank and the IMF. Regulation and taxation of speculative capital and a strictly enforced Code of Conduct for TNCs is therefore needed.

6. Social Peace
Everyone has the right to be free from violence. Food must not be used as a weapon. Increasing levels of poverty and marginalization in the countryside, along with the growing oppression of ethnic minorities and indigenous populations aggravate situations of injustice and hopelessness. The ongoing displacement, forced urbanisation, repression and increasing incidence of racism of smallholder farmers cannot be tolerated.

7. Democratic Control

Smallholder farmers must have direct input into formulating agricultural policies at all levels. The United Nations and related organizations will have to undergo a process of democratization to enable this to become a reality. Everyone has the right to honest, accurate information and open and democratic decision-making. These rights form the basis of good governance, accountability and equal participation in economic, political and social life, free from all forms of discrimination. Rural women, in particular, must be granted direct and active decision-making on food and rural issues.

In other texts, Via Campesina gives more acknowledgement to the recognition of women farmers' rights, who play a major role in agricultural and food production. It can be either subsumed under the seven headlines or be seen as an eighth core principle.

From Rome to Cancun – NGO/CSO discussion forums and activities linked to Food Sovereignty

Since 1996 the concept of Food Sovereignty has been used by social movements, NGOs and CSOs in parallel NGO-fora both to the World Food Summit, the WFS:*fyl*, and other events. Through these fora the concept has gradually become a major issue in international agricultural debate, as it is also within the United Nations bodies and among some official decision-makers.

Since 1996, when Via Campesina outlined the seven principles for Food Sovereignty, the principles suggested by civil society have to a great extent remained the same. However, over time these principles have become more comprehensive and have been formulated into more concrete policy objectives.

Core documents on the development of the concept of Food Sovereignty

In relation to the forums and activities that have taken place since 1996, a number of papers and documents have been published (Table 3). Most of the literature has emerged during the last five years and has been published by civil society.

Table 3: Overview of the core documents on Food Sovereignty

Statements and declarations

Date of publication	Title	Author/location
April 1996	'Tlaxcala Declaration of the Via Campesina'	Via Campesina, Tlaxcala, Mexico
November 1996	'The right to produce and the access to land. Food Sovereignty: A Future without Hunger'	Via Campesina, Rome, Italy
	'Profit for a few or food for all'	Rome, Italy
November 1996	'WTO – Shrink or Sink!'	Our World is Not for Sale Network
March 2000	'End Hunger! Fight for the Right to Live'	Asian regional Consultation, Bangkok, Thailand
August 2001	'Our World is Not for Sale. WTO: Shrink or Sink'	Our World is Not for Sale Network

Date of publication	Title	Author/location
August 2001	'Final Declaration of the World Forum on Food Sovereignty'	Havana, Cuba
September 2001	'Priority to Peoples' Food Sovereignty'	Via Campesina
November 2001	'End World Hunger – Commit to Food Sovereignty'	Kathmandu, Nepal
May 2002	'Food Sovereignty: A Right for All. Political Statement of the NGO/CSO Forum for Food Sovereignty'	Rome, Italy
June 2002	'Statement on People's Food Sovereignty: Our world is not for sale. Priority to Peoples' Food Sovereignty. WTO out of Food and Agriculture'	Cancun, Mexico
September 2003	'Statement on People's Food Sovereignty: Our world is not for sale. Priority to Peoples' Food Sovereignty. WTO out of Food and Agriculture'	Cancun, Mexico

Papers:

Date of publication	Title	Author/location
November 2001	'Sale of the Century? Peoples Food Sovereignty. Part 1 – the implications of current trade negotiations'	Friends of the Earth International, Amsterdam, the Netherlands
November 2001	'Sale of the Century? Peoples Food Sovereignty' Part 2 – a new multilateral framework for food and agriculture'	Friends of the Earth International
November 2001	'Food Sovereignty in the Era of Trade Liberalization: Are Multilateral Means Feasible?'	Suppan, S. Institute for Agriculture and Trade Policy (IATP)
June 2002	'Sustaining Agricultural Biodiversity and the integrity and free flow of Genetic Resources for Food for Agriculture'	ETC/GRAIN/ITDG
January 2003	'What is Food Sovereignty?'	Via Campesina
February 2003	'Towards Food Sovereignty: Constructing and Alternative to the World Trade Organization's Agreement on Agriculture Farmers, Food and Trade'	International Workshop on the Review of the AoA. Geneva, Switzerland
April 2003	'Trade and People's Food Sovereignty'	Friends of the Earth
June 2003	'How TRIPs threatens biodiversity and Food Sovereignty' Conclusions and recommendations from NGO perspectives.	Hyderabad, India

The majority of the literature consists of position papers which are very much in line with the statements and declarations presented in this paper. In this regard two position papers were published in 2001: *'Priority to Peoples' Food Sovereignty'* by Via Campesina, and *'Sale of the Century? Peoples Food Sovereignty'*, published in two parts by Friends of the Earth. The latter outlines a detailed proposal for a new multilateral framework for food and agriculture. Both position papers follow the principles described in this paper and are therefore not repeated here.

Food Sovereignty in the Era of Trade Liberalization: Are Multilateral Means Feasible?

For the NGO Forum for Food Sovereignty, 2002, the paper *'Food Sovereignty in the Era of Trade Liberalization: Are Multilateral Means Feasible?'*, was prepared by Steve Suppan, from the Institute for Agriculture and Trade Policy (IATP), based in Minneapolis. This paper evaluates some of the policies that have been adopted by civil society in order to achieve Food Sovereignty. The policy proposals discussed are:

- the establishment of global or regional basic commodity reserves in relation to GMOs in food aid;
- a Global Food Security Convention; and
- WTO commitments to phase out dumping of agricultural products.

Considering the global food security convention, Suppan argues that such a convention would evidently meet great resistance since it implies that food security would have the highest priority within international food policy. The interests of governments in using agricultural export revenues to pay international creditors, the financial interests of international trading countries with minimum market access guaranteed by the AoA, and the interests of governments to use food as part of their diplomatic arsenals, would all be affected by the realisation of such a convention, Suppan maintains. When it comes to how the WTO might contribute to Food Sovereignty by phasing out dumping of agricultural commodities, Suppan suggests that agricultural dumping by states should be determined by comparing the export price to the exporting countries' full cost of production. An annual report by the major exporting countries could therefore facilitate the phasing-out of dumping. Even though agriculture dumping is by no means the only cause of the difficult situation the rural poor are facing, governments would seriously have to consider the effects of these policies, Suppan concludes.

Sustaining Agricultural Biodiversity

'Sustaining Agricultural Biodiversity' (2002), written by the ETC Group, GRAIN, and ITDG, is another document that was prepared for the WFS:*fyl* NGO/CSO Forum for Food Sovereignty. These organizations focus more on agricultural biodiversity and the question of access to genetic resources for food and agriculture. With that paper they highlight an additional aspect of the Food Sovereignty debate, which is of central importance to the definition and the conceptual background, namely the agricultural model of production. In this background paper the organizations challenge the industrial model of agriculture because of its negative impact on agricultural biodiversity:

'Since the dawn of agriculture 12,000 years ago, humans have nurtured plants and animals to provide food. Careful selection of the traits, tastes and textures that make good food resulted in a myriad diversity of genetic resources, varieties, breeds and sub-species of the relatively few plants and animals humans use for food and agriculture

– agricultural biodiversity. Agricultural biodiversity also includes the diversity of species that support production – soil biota, pollinators, predators and so on – and those species in the wider environment that support diverse agroecosystems – agricultural, pastoral, forest and aquatic ecosystems. These diverse varieties, breeds and systems underpin food security and provide insurance against future threats, adversity and ecological changes.

Agricultural biodiversity is the first link in the food chain, developed and safeguarded by indigenous peoples, and women and men farmers, forest dwellers, livestock keepers and fisherfolk throughout the world. It has developed as a result of the free flow of genetic resources between food producers.

Agricultural biodiversity is now under threat. Animal breeds, plant varieties and the genetic resources they contain are being eroded at an alarming rate. More than 90% of crop varieties have been lost from farmers' fields in the past century and livestock breeds are disappearing at the rate of 5% per year and aquatic life is similarly threatened. Soil biodiversity including microbial diversity and the diversity of pollinators and predators are also under serious threat. Urgent actions are needed to reverse these trends in situ and on-farm. Also there is a need to implement actions to protect the genetic resources stored in ex situ *public genebanks, which are often poorly maintained. Threats to these resources, both in situ and ex situ, also include pollution by genetically modified material and the increasing use of intellectual property rights (IPRs) to claim sole ownership over varieties, breeds and genes, which thereby restricts access for farmers and other food producers. This loss of diversity is exacerbating food insecurity that today sends more than 1.2 billion people to bed hungry. The discourse on Access to Genetic Resources is thus wider than concerns at a genetic level. It should be widened to include all of agricultural biodiversity, for it is the whole interdependent complex, developed through human activity in natural resource management for food and agricultural, livestock and fisheries production, that is under threat.'*

In order to preserve agricultural biodiversity and guarantee Food Sovereignty three international agreements in particular were seen as important. The first is the FAO *International Treaty on Plant Genetic Resources for Food and Agriculture* (IT PGRFA). Such an agreement should, for example, ensure the right to save, sell and exchange seeds. It would require the implementation of a clause that prohibits claims of intellectual property rights, outlawing biopiracy of these resources, and ensuring rights and rewards to farmers.

The second agreement is the *Leipzig Global Plan Action on Plant Genetic Resources for Food and Agriculture* that could facilitate the implementation of existing FAO agreements, decisions and the Convention on Biological Diversity (CBD). This would include the Agricultural Biodiversity Decisions of the CBD, relevant FAO Conference decisions, and Commitment 3 of the WFS's Plan of Action on sustainable agriculture. These agreements would, according to the authors, enable improved conservation and sustainable use of plant genetic resources for food and agriculture and contribute to reversing the decline in agricultural biodiversity.

Thirdly, it is argued that genetic resources could be given some protection by mandatory decisions of the CBD, which would include the implementation of the *Cartagena Protocol on Biosafety* that would oblige owners of the intellectual property rights of GMOs to provide compensation for any damaging outcomes resulting from GMOs in food, seeds and livestock breeds, grains or the environment.[29]

How TRIPs threatens biodiversity and Food Sovereignty

Another paper that deals particularly with biodiversity as a means to Food Sovereignty is '*How TRIPs threatens biodiversity and Food Sovereignty*'. The paper is an outcome of the NGO/CSO meeting in Hyderabad, India in June 2003. The paper gives a number of concrete proposals for policy changes on how to guarantee bio-diversity and calls upon national governments to introduce and enforce an alternative national/international legal framework outside the WTO setting that would safeguard the communities' rights and control over resources. Moreover, it suggests ensuring that WTO rules do not undermine national/international legal frameworks outside the WTO setting.

Towards Food Sovereignty: Constructing an Alternative to the World Trade Organization's Agreement on Agriculture

Another document published in 2003 was '*Towards Food Sovereignty: Constructing an Alternative to the World Trade Organization's Agreement on Agriculture*', which emanated from a working group of civil society smallholder farmers' groups participating at a Farmers, Food and Trade International Workshop on the review of the AoA in Geneva in February, 2003. This document benefited from a number of statements and declarations already made by NGOs and CSOs, and therefore offered a thorough overview of civil society positions. The paper outlined four articles in constructing an alternative agreement on agriculture. Among measures to end dumping of agricultural commodities, the establishment of import control and price bands were discussed. It stated that countries should be encouraged to implement price band systems or variable import levels to stabilize internal prices for agricultural commodities. These measures would stabilize rural economies by regulating the volatility of import entry prices and prevent unfair undercutting of domestic agricultural prices caused by dumping, the authors argued. Moreover, measures to curtail the practice of food aid being used as a dumping mechanism were discussed. In addition to the Cartagena Protocol on Biosafety and the International Treaty on Plant Genetic Resources for Food and Agriculture, the importance of the implementation of international marine agreements and conventions such as the *UN Fish Stocks Agreement* were highlighted. The efficient implementation of these conventions would help countries to protect national and international agricultural and aquatic resources from both land-based and sea-based threats, such as pollution, mineral extraction, and degradation, the authors concluded.

Other documents

Other documents that were published in 2003 were '*What is Food Sovereignty?*', where Via Campesina reaffirmed its position and '*Trade and people's Food Sovereignty*' published in April by Friends of the Earth. In preparation for the WTO meeting in Cancun in September, a number of position papers were published by different civil society groups. Among these, the article '*A Constructive Approach towards Agriculture, Food and Water in Cancun*', written by Mark Ritchie of IATP, offered a set of policy objectives that were representative of a broad majority of civil society groups. The article presented five specific trade policy objectives that he suggested would form the basis for civil society groups. The policies outlined were ending dumping, and defending Fair Trade, (i.e. ensuring the prices paid to farmers and charged to consumers were fair and reflected the full cost of production, including environmental protection and social justice). Ritchie emphasized the importance of promoting international commodity agreements as a way to structure and balance the supply and demand at the global level, particularly in the light of record low prices in commodities like coffee and cotton. Moreover, Ritchie stressed the importance of preventing the monopolization and control over food supplies and maintaining public control over water in order to achieve Food Sovereignty. According to Ritchie, the most efficient way to achieve these five objectives would be to build on a partnership between civil society and supportive governments.

Peoples' Convention on Food Sovereignty

Asian civil society organizations published a draft of a *'Peoples' Convention on Food Sovereignty'*[30] in July 2004. In the second paragraph of the preamble it says: *'By this Convention, Food Sovereignty becomes the right of people and communities to decide and implement their agricultural and food policies and strategies for sustainable production and distribution of food. It is the right to adequate, safe, nutritional and culturally appropriate food and to produce food sustainably and ecologically. It is the right to access of productive resources such as land, water, seeds and biodiversity for sustainable utilization'.*

The draft was released at the time of the People's Caravan for Food Sovereignty. It was meant to be an advocacy manifesto for all the people's movements, and to result in a concerted demands for governmental policy changes. The draft has 15 articles, which cover issues such as access to food, genuine agrarian reform, food safety, etc. The structure is quite similar to that of the Voluntary Guidelines for the implementation of the right to adequate food, which were adopted by FAO member states in November, 2004.

Literature overview

This literature overview indicates that the underlying concern about the need for the principles of Food Sovereignty remains unchanged, irrespective of author or text. What changes are the elements that are highlighted or which issues are the focus of each of the texts. They all start with the recognition that substantive policy changes are needed in order to overcome the problems of hunger and poverty. Five issues are covered in all the texts:

1. The term Food Sovereignty refers to a combination of national and international policies that need to be changed. Even if the term sovereignty seems to focus on the international dimension of the problem, and most authors do the same, all definitions also refer, nevertheless, to necessary national changes, particularly concerning access to land.

2. Most of the concept papers focus on trade policy instruments. The need for substantial changes here is crucial.

3. Linked to this is a third focus that can be found in nearly all the texts, and that is access to agricultural inputs, particularly the sovereignty over seeds and livestock breeds. The commercialization of the core and starting point of all kinds of agriculture, particularly through intellectual property rights, is an issue that concerns different NGOs/CSOs and is strongly rejected in all papers.

4. A fourth focus in almost all the texts is a rejection of all forms of monopolisation.

5. Privatization is also condemned, and described as leading to a process in which public resources such as drinking water can be monopolized.

To address these issues, all texts contain policy proposals that differ a lot more than the analyses of the problems in those texts; analyses converge, while proposed corrective measures diverge. Some texts propose far-reaching changes in international agreements ('agriculture out of WTO', for example), others propose new international legal instruments for the governance of food and agriculture, while still others suggest using the existing instruments but making them more responsive to the needs of the poor and hungry.

Literature and references

Alston, P. and K. Tomasevski (1984) *The Right to Food*. Stichting Studie en Informatiecentrum Mensenrechten – SIM, Martinus Nijhof Publishers, Leiden, The Netherlands.

Altieri, Miguel A. (1995) *Agroecology: The Science of Sustainable Agriculture*. IT Publications, London.

Altieri, Miguel A. (2002) 'Agroecology: The science of natural resources management for poor farmers in marginal environments', in *Agriculture, Ecosystems and Environment 1971*, p.1–24, Elsevier.

BMVEL (2004) *Ernährungs und agrarpolitischer Bericht 2004 der Bundesregierung*. Bundesministerium für Verbraucherschutz, Ernährung und Landwirtschaft (BMWEL), Berlin.

Brown, L. (2003) *Vital Signs 2003*. World Watch Institute, Washington.

Cartagena Protocol on Biosafety (no date) Text of the Protocol. Article 2. General Provisions. www.biodiv.org/biosafety/articles.asp?lg=0&a=bsp-02

Christian Aid (1999) *Taking stock: How the supermarkets stack up on ethical trading*. www.christian-aid.org.uk/indepth/9902stoc/stock1.htm

CIOEC (2003) 'Towards a World Convention on Food Sovereignty and Trade'. Coordinadora de Integración de Organizaciones Económicas campesinas de Bolivia, (CIOEC), www.cioecbolivia.org/wgt/food_sovereignty.htm

Convention on Biological Diversity (1996) Recommendation III/3. www.biodiv.org/recommendations/default.asp?m=sbstta-03&r=03&print=1

Convention on Biological Diversity (2002) Agricultural biological diversity DecisionVI/5. www.biodiv.org/decisions/default.asp?lg=0&dec=VI/5

Eide, A., A. Oshaug and W.B. Eide (1991) 'Food Security and the Right to Food in International Law and development', in *Transnational Law & Contemporary Problems Vol.1 No.2*, University of Iowa.

'End Hunger! Fight for the Right to Live' (2001) NGOs/CSOs Statement in the Asian Regional Consultation on the World Food Summit:*fyl*. Bangkok, Thailand. August, 2001. www.fao.org/tc/NGO/region/Asia_en.htm

'End World Hunger – Commit to Food Sovereignty' (2002) Asian NGO/CSO Declaration to the World Food Summit:*fyl*. Kathmandu, Nepal. May, 2002. www.fao.org/tc/NGO/region/KathmanduDeclaration_en.htm

ETC/GRAIN/ITDG (2002) 'Sustaining Agricultural Biodiversity and the Integrity and Free Flow of Genetic Resources for Food for Agriculture'. www.ukabc.org/accessgenres.pdf

European Parliament (2002) 'Draft opinion of the Committee on Women's Rights and Equal Opportunities for the Committee on Development and Cooperation on health and poverty reduction in developing countries, November 13'. www.europarl.eu.int/meetdocs/committees/femm/20021125/482141en.pdf

FAO (1983a) *Approaches to World Food Security, Economic and Social Development Paper No.32.* FAO, Rome.

FAO (1983b) *Progress in Implementation of the Plan of Action to Strengthen World Food Security.* C/83/29. FAO, Rome.

FAO (1996) *Rome Declaration on World Food Security and World Food Summit Plan of Action.* Document WFS 96/3, FAO, Rome.

FAO (2001) 'High-Level Panel on Resource Mobilisation for Food Security and for Agriculture and Rural Development'. World Food Summit:*fyl*, Rome, June, 2001.

FAO (2002a) *International Alliance against Hunger.* FAO, Rome.

FAO (2002b) 'Biodiversity and the Ecosystem Approach in Agriculture, Forestry and Fisheries'. Proceedings of the Satellite Event on the occasion of the Ninth Regular Session of the Commission on Genetic Resources for Food and Agriculture. FAO, Rome, 2002.

FAO (2003a) *World Agriculture 2015/2030.* FAO, Rome.

FAO (2003b) 'Climate change and agriculture: Physical and human dimension', in *World Agriculture 2015/2030*, Chapter 13. FAO, Rome.

FAO (2003c) *The State of Food Insecurity in the World 2003.* FAO, Rome, November 2003.

FAO (2004a) *The State of Food Insecurity in the World 2004.* FAO, Rome, November 2004.

FAO (2004b) 'Voluntary Guidelines for the progressive realization of the right to adequate food in the context of national food security'. September, 2004 (IGWG RTFG 5/REP 1). www.fao.org/righttofood/common/ecg/51596_en_VGS_eng_web.pdf

FAO Committee on World Food Security (2003) The Anti Hunger Program. 29th Session. FAO, Rome, May 12–16. www.fao.org/DOCREP/004/Y6684E/Y6684E00.HTM

FARM (2004) 'CAP Reforms fudge real issues behind farming exodus'. www.farm.org.uk/FM_Content.aspx?ID=169

'Final Declaration of the World Forum on Food Sovereignty', Havana, Cuba, 7 September, 2001. www.ukabc.org/havanadeclaration.pdf

Friends of the Earth International (2001a) *Sale of the Century? Peoples Food Sovereignty. Part 1 – the implications of current trade negotiations.* www.foe.co.uk/resource/reports/qatar_food_sovereignty_1.pdf

Friends of the Earth International (2001b) *Sale of the Century? Peoples Food Sovereignty' Part 2 – A new multilateral framework for food and agriculture.* www.foe.co.uk/resource/reports/qatar_food_sovereignty_2.pdf

Friends of the Earth International (2003) *Trade and People's Food Sovereignty.* www.foei.org/publications/trade/newfinallowres.pdf

Haddad, L. and S. Gillespie (2001) 'Effective food and nutrition policy response to HIV/AIDS: What we know and what we need to know', *Discussion Paper No.112*, IFPRI, Washington, D.C.

Hines, Colin (2003) *A Global Look to the Local. Replacing economic globalization with democratic localization.* IIED, London.

'How TRIPs threatens biodiversity and Food Sovereignty' (2003) Conclusions and recommendations from NGO perspectives. Hyderabad, India, 18–21 June. www.eed.de/fix/files/Internetversion%20englisch.pdf

IAGW-FIVIMS (2000) 'Guidelines for national FIVIMS. Background and principles'. Inter-agency Working Group on FIVIMS, FAO, Rome,

IATP (ed) (2003) *Towards Food Sovereignty: Constructing an Alternative to the World Trade Organization's Agreement on Agriculture Farmers, Food and Trade.* International Workshop on the Review of the AoA. Geneva, February. www.tradeobservatory.org/library/uploadedfiles/Towards_Food_Sovereignty_Constructing_an_Alter.pdf

IFAD (2001) *Rural Poverty Report 2001. The Challenge of Ending Rural Poverty.* IFAD, Rome.

Kent, G. (2001) 'Food and Trade Rights', *UN Chronicle, Issue 3.* www.un.org/Pubs/chronicle/2002/issue1/0102p27.html

Künnenmann, R. (2002) 'Food Security: Evading the Human Right to Food?', *FIAN Magazine No.1*, Berlin.

Mulvany, Patrick (2002) 'Hunger, a gnawing shame. Report from World Food Summit:*fyl*'. www.ukabc.org/wfs5+report.pdf

Murphy, S. (1999) 'Market Power in Agricultural Markets: Some Issues for Developing Countries', *T.R.A.D.E. Working Paper 6*, South Centre, Geneva. www.southcentre.org/publications/agric/wto6.pdf

Murphy, S. (2002) *Managing the Invisible Hand: Markets, Farmers and International Trade.* Institute for Agriculture and Trade Policy (IATP), Minneapolis. www.wtowatch.org/library/admin/uploadedfiles/Managing_the_Invisible_Hand_2.pdf

Negotiating Group on Agriculture (1988) MTN.GNG/NG5/W/86. Special Distribution. Summary of the main points raised at the eleventh meeting of the negotiation group on agriculture. November 10.

Our World is Not for Sale Network (2001) *WTO: Shrink or Sink.* Our World is not for Sale Network, June, 2001. www.ourworldisnotforsale.org/statements.asp

NGO Forum to the World Food Summit (1996) 'Profit for a few or food for all? Food Sovereignty and Security to Eliminate the Globalization of Hunger, A Statement by the NGO Forum to the World Food Summit'. Rome, 17 November. www.rlc.fao.org/ong/cuba/pdf/02apoeng.pdf

NGO/CSO Forum for Food Sovereignty (2002) 'Food Sovereignty: A Right for All. Political Statement of the NGO/CSO Forum for Food Sovereignty'. Rome, 13 June. www.croceviaterra.it/FORUM/DOCUMENTI%20DEL%20FORUM/political%20statement.pdf

Oxfam International (2002) *Rigged Rules and Double Standards: Trade globalization, and the fight against poverty.* Oxfam International, Oxford.

People's Food Sovereignty Network (2002) www.peoplesfoodsovereignty.org/statements/new%20statement/statement_01.htm

People's Food Sovereignty Network (2003) 'Statement on People's Food Sovereignty: Our world is not for sale'. Cancun, 10–14 September, 2003. www.peoplesfoodsovereignty.org/statements/state_wto_agri_eng/1.htm

People's Food Sovereignty Network (2004) 'Beijing Declaration from NGO/CSO Regional Consultation: From Agenda to Action'. Follow-up to the NGO/CSO Forum for Food Sovereignty. www.peoplesfoodsovereignty.org/statements/new/23.htm

People's Food Sovereignty Network Asia Pacific and Pesticide Action Network Asia and the Pacific (2004) *Primer on People's Food Sovereignty* and *Draft People's Convention on Food Sovereignty*. www.panap.net

Population Reference Bureau (2003) *World Population Data Sheet*. Washington D.C, July 2003.

Pretty, Jules (2001) 'Reducing Food Poverty with Sustainable Agriculture: A Summary of New Evidence' http://www2.essex.ac.uk/ces/ResearchProgrammes/SAFEWexecsummfinalreport. htm

Pretty, Jules and Parviz Koohafkan (2002) *Land and Agriculture: from UNCED, Rio de Janeiro 1992 to WSSD, Johannesburg 2002: A compendium of recent sustainable development initiatives in the field of agriculture and land management*. FAO, Rome.

Prove, P.N. (2003) *Human rights in trade and investment agreements: The legal framework of economic globalization, and the right to food*. Lutheran World Federation, Geneva.

Ritchie, M. (2003) *A Constructive Approach towards Agriculture, Food and Water in Cancun*. Institute for Agriculture and Trade Policy (IATP), Minnesota, USA www.tradeobservatory.org/library/uploadedfiles/Constructive_Approach_towards _Agriculture_Food.htm

Scialabba, Nadia El-Hage and Caroline Hattam (eds) (2002) 'Organic agriculture, environment and food security', *Environment and Natural Resources Series, No.4.* FAO, Rome, 2002.

Sen, A. (1981) *Poverty and Famines: An Essay on Entitlement and Deprivation*. Clarendon Press, Oxford.

Short, C. (2000) 'Sustainable Food Security for All by 2020. Food Insecurity: A Symptom of Poverty'. Department for International Development (DFID), London. www.ifpri.org/2020conference/PDF/summary_short.pdf

SLE (2002) 'Integration of Food and Nutrition Security in Poverty Reduction Strategy Papers (PRSPs). A case study of Ethiopia, Mozambique, Rwanda and Uganda'. Centre for advanced training in rural development of the Humboldt-University in Berlin (SLE), Berlin, December 2002.

Spitz, P. (2002) 'Food Security, the right to food and the FAO', in *FIAN-Magazine 01/02.*

Suppan, S. (2001) *Food Sovereignty in the Era of Trade Liberalization: Are Multilateral Means Feasible?* IATP, Geneva. www.rlc.fao.org/ong/cuba/pdf/02ofieng.pdf

SUSTAIN (2003) *Feeding the Future: Policy options for local food – A discussion paper*. SUSTAIN, London.

UK Food Group (2003) *Food, Inc.: Corporate concentration from farm to consumer*. London. www.ukfg.org.uk/docs/UKFG-Foodinc-Nov03.pdf

UNDP (2003a) *Halving Global Hunger, Background Paper of Task Force on Hunger.* UNDP, New York. www.unmillenniumproject.org/documents/tf02apr18.pdf

UNDP (2003b) *The Millennium Project. Hunger Task Force Report.* UNDP, New York, April 2003.

UNDP (2005) *The Millennium Project 2005. Halving Hunger: It Can Be Done.* Final Report of the Task Force on Hunger. The Earth Institute at Columbia University, New York. www.unmillenniumproject.org/who/tf2docs.htm

Via Campesina (1996a) 'Tlaxcala Declaration of the Via Campesina', Tlaxcala, Mexico, 18–21 April, www.virtualsask.com/via/lavia.deceng.html

Via Campesina (1996b) 'Food Sovereignty: A Future without Hunger', Rome, 11–17 November. www.viacampesina.org/imprimer.php3?id_article=38

Via Campesina (2001) 'Priority to Peoples' Food Sovereignty'. 1 November. www.viacampesina.org/IMG/_article_PDF/article_34.pdf

Via Campesina (2003) 'What is Food Sovereignty?' 1 January. www.viacampesina.org/IMG/_article_PDF/article_216.pdf

Walelign, T. (2002) 'The 5th P7 Summit: Food Sovereignty and Democracy: Let the world feed itself', in *GREEN/EFA International Relations Newsletter, No 6*, December 2002. Brussels, Belgium.

WFC (ed.) (1983) *Food Security for People – Direct Measures to Reduce Hunger*, UN Doc. WFC/1982/6.

Windfuhr, M. (2002) 'Food Security, Food Sovereignty, Right to Food. Competing or complementary approaches to fight hunger and malnutrition?' *Hungry for what is Right, FIAN Magazine, No 1.*

Windfuhr, M. (2003) 'Food Sovereignty and the Right to Adequate Food'. *Discussion Paper 2003*, FIAN, Germany.

'World Food Summit: *Five Years Later*: Food and Agriculture Organization of the United Nations'. A Selection of NGO Perspectives (2002) Rome, June 2002. www.casin.ch/pdf/wfs5.pdf

World Watch Institute (2003) *Vital Signs 2003*, Washington, DC.

'WTO – Shrink or Sink!' The Turnaround Agenda International Civil Society Sign-On Letter (2000) March 2000. www.citizen.org/trade/wto/shrink_sink/article

March 7, 2007

March 7, 2007